Understanding Oil Prices

For other titles in the Wiley Finance series
please see www.wiley.com/finance

Understanding Oil Prices

A Guide to What Drives the Price of Oil in Today's Markets

Salvatore Carollo

WILEY

A John Wiley & Sons, Ltd., Publication

This edition first published 2012
© 2012 Salvatore Carollo

Registered office
John Wiley & Sons Ltd, The Atrium, Southern Gate, Chichester, West Sussex, PO19 8SQ,
United Kingdom

For details of our global editorial offices, for customer services and for information about how to
apply for permission to reuse the copyright material in this book please see our website at
www.wiley.com.

Wiley publishes in a variety of print and electronic formats and by print-on-demand. Some
material included with standard print versions of this book may not be included in e-books or in
print-on-demand. If this book refers to media such as a CD or DVD that is not included in the
version you purchased, you may download this material at http://booksupport.wiley.com. For
more information about Wiley products, visit us at www.wiley.com.

Designations used by companies to distinguish their products are often claimed as trademarks.
All brand names and product names used in this book are trade names, service marks, trademarks
or registered trademarks of their respective owners. The publisher is not associated with any
product or vendor mentioned in this book. This publication is designed to provide accurate and
authoritative information in regard to the subject matter covered. It is sold on the understanding
that the publisher is not engaged in rendering professional services. If professional advice or other
expert assistance is required, the services of a competent professional should be sought.

Library of Congress Cataloging-in-Publication Data
Carollo, Salvatore.
    Understanding oil prices : a guide to what drives the price of oil in today's markets / Salvatore
Carollo.
        p. cm.—(The wiley finance series)
    Includes bibliographical references and index.
    ISBN 978-1-119-96272-4 (hardback)
    1. Petroleum products—Prices.   2. Petroleum industry and trade—History.   I. Title.
    HD9560.4.C37   2012
    338.2'3282—dc23

                                                                                          2011039266

A catalogue record for this book is available from the British Library.

ISBN 978-1-119-96272-4 (hardback) ISBN 978-1-119-96289-2 (ebk)
ISBN 978-1-119-96290-8 (ebk)   ISBN 978-1-119-96291-5 (ebk)

Set in 11/13pt Times by Aptara Inc., New Delhi, India
Printed in Great Britain by TJ International Ltd, Padstow, Cornwall, UK

A Sofia e Riccardo

Parmi d'aver per lunghe esperienze osservato
tale essere la condizione umana
intorno alle cose intellettuali,
che quanto altri meno ne intende e ne sa,
tanto più risolutamente voglia discorrerne;
e che, all'incontro, la moltitudine delle cose conosciute ed intese
renda più lento e irresoluto al sentenziare circa qualche novità.

It seems to me, after long experience
in observing the human condition
as regards intellectual matters,
that some persons, the less they understand and know,
all the more forcibly wish to hold forth;
and that, when we encounter something new,
the myriad things known and understood
make any judgement regarding it slower and less conclusive.

Galileo Galilei

Contents

Foreword

This book was conceived after a critical re-reading of the lectures I gave at the Eni Corporate University (ECU) for the Master MEDEA and for the Annual Seminar on oil marketing.

It is therefore the result not only of my elaborations and market models developed over the years to interpret the international oil market, but also of the discussions in the lecture hall with the students of the Master MEDEA and with the representatives of those producing countries who have taken part in the various editions of the Annual Seminar.

My thanks are due above all to these persons.

I also wish to thank Prof. Enzo Di Giulio, president of ECU, who desired to be present in these lectures and encouraged me to put the content of my presentations in book form.

Finally, I owe particular thanks to Dr Caterina Marmorato who, apart from helping me with notable professional commitment in the delivery of the lectures for the Master course, dedicated a good part of her free time for several months in preparing the technical annexes and in the task of editing.

Preface

The title of the book you are holding – *Understanding Oil Prices: A Guide to What Drives Oil Prices in Today's Markets* – brings to mind the telling of a story. Now, we know that for a story to be a good story it should meet three conditions: a) there are certain events to relate; b) these events run in order, that is, their sequence has some sense and, if possible, succeeds in holding the attention of the reader; c) there is a voice that narrates the story effectively and clearly. We feel that Salvatore Carollo's book satisfies all three of these conditions, and it tells a story of great interest to all of us.

The world of oil seems to be cloaked by a form of disparity in comprehension. Without oil, our entire existence – as we know it today – would not be possible. Despite the countless discussions regarding the oil peak and the end of the oil era, this fuel still represents, by far, the primary energy source. According to the last World Energy Outlook of the IEA, the proportion of oil as a source of energy stands at 34% against the 26% of coal and 21% of gas. According to the IMF's World Economic Outlook (WEO) reference scenario, in 2030 it will still be the primary source: 30% as against the 29% of coal and 22% of gas. Oil has, and continues to have, a profound influence on the lives of westerners and perhaps even more so on that of the peoples of the east. Certainly, it is a non-renewable source and this means that its days, in the long term, are numbered. But that is not the point here: the heart of the matter is that we are dealing with a material that shapes, changes, models, directs and configures the history of the world. And this is destined to carry on for a long time – true even when the lusty flames of oil, ephemeral like all the things in this world, fade away in the great emptiness of time. Just as the Hellenistic or Roman worlds still influence

our lives despite their decline – consider for a moment our language –
in the same way, oil has given the world a development and geopolitical
model, which is destined to last for the coming centuries. But this is
the future. Today, rather, we are in the midst of the oil era. And yet,
as we said earlier, there is a depressingly inadequate awareness of the
significance of this essential source. This very book has come to your
hands, reader, thanks to oil. Here we are not talking about a technical
knowledge of the complex work of exploration, or oilfield production,
or of the transport of crude oil across the oceans of the globe. Rather,
we refer to those three words that millions, if not billions, of times
stand out in the media: the 'price of oil'. This expression, the content
of which has such a powerful influence on our lives, is the synthesis of
immense forces – costs, decisions regarding investments and expenses,
use of reserves, operations to cover risks, speculations, transactions, the
policies of contracting companies, the policies of nations, oil companies
and so on – that interact to form it. At the same time, from the price
itself stem innumerable chains of actions that influence variables of
fundamental importance for the entire economy: the quotations of the
dollar and the euro, the balance of payments, the price of gasoline and
gasoil, the cost of electricity, the rate of inflation, employment and so on.
Thus, the price of oil has a vast and forceful impact on our existence.
And despite all this, the issue is not adequately discussed. Rather, it
is mentioned, hinted at and at times journalists try to explain it; but
beyond the inner circle of specialists no one talks much about it. And
this circle, to tell the truth, is very restricted. This is a destiny that oil
shares, unfortunately, with all the sources of energy. Just reflect on the
scarce availability of courses in energy economics in universities across
the world. A similar reflection applies to books on energy economics
that are a *rara avis* on this planet, particularly if we compare them
with the plethora of texts on environmental economics. Paradoxically,
energy – which represents perhaps the central axle around which the
entire economy rotates – is almost never an issue to dissect in our degree
courses, in particular those regarding economics. Thus, tethered within
the strict boundaries of a territory for specialists, the price of oil remains
an abstruse, esoteric matter. When an attempt is made to pass from the
esoteric to the exoteric, it is often done in a misguided, amateurish way.
The media advances information that evokes horrific scenarios – until
last year some were predicting a price of around \$200 per barrel – they
talk of an oil peak and the end of oil. Alternatively, OPEC is indicted as

being responsible for the high prices, inflating its role disproportionately. In this way, public opinion tends to form biased opinions based on explanations that draw attention to just one main force, as the only one responsible for what happens.

This book by Salvatore Carollo speaks of all this. It tells a story, as we said, and it does so starting from the end, namely the crude oil price collapse of last year from almost $150 to under $40 per barrel. Why did this happen? To what extent can the fundamentals explain it? Starting from these questions, the book offers an examination of the phenomenon that takes us nimbly through the essential phases of the evolution of crude oil price. The volume deals with relevant aspects – some quite technical – such as purchase contracts, the structure of world supply, the evolution of environmental regulations and, naturally, the refining process for crude oil. But at its core remains the key question of the price and its formation. The various issues discussed serve as fodder for the exploration of the primary question, as if they were pieces of a jigsaw to be completed. Certainly, as regards the role of the various forces that drive prices up or down, the book offers a very clear explanation. In one sense, it tracks down some of those guilty. We will not reveal them here, so as not to deprive the readers of the pleasure of discovering them in due course. We will only declare that the text materializes from the vast experiences of the author. As we read, we hear the voice of a professional, namely a man who works in the oil arena and whose main task is, for his part, to contribute towards the formation of prices, and not explain them. And yet, the author belongs to that class of professionals that master, thanks to their deliberation, whatever they do, in this way succeeding to unify thought with action. Unfortunately, their class is very rare: it is hard to say whether it is more or less rare than that of the academic who follows the inverse route, passing from theory to practice. What is certain is that the marriage of practice and reflection has produced a stimulating and enjoyable book. Some readers will appreciate its structure, which alternates the narration with the technical aspects, others the voice, still others will find it an interesting and nimble introduction to the world of oil, and others, finally, may see it as a sort of text book. Some will agree with its propositions, others not: we can be certain of that. But the function of a book is precisely this: to stimulate reflection and nurture knowledge with thought. To quote the celebrated words of a troubled writer of the 1900s, Franz Kafka – as troubled as the oil market! – 'a book must be a pickaxe for the frozen sea that resides within us'. And the frozen sea is not only the existential and interior one as navigated by the writer from Prague. Often, the ice on the sea is created by prejudices, the knowledge fossilized inside us and never seen again, by the ready-made explanations, by their nebulosity which is never questioned. This book has the honour and duty to be a robust pickaxe.

Enzo Di Giulio
President, Scuola Enrico Mattei

Quick Reference Guide

To assist the reader a glossary of the technical terms that have been only briefly considered in the text has been added. Other terms have been described in some detail in the pertinent chapters.

- **ASSESSMENT:** this term is used in the text to mean estimate and/or valuation.
- **AUTHOR'S SOURCE:** when this reference is indicated, the source of data and graphs should be intended as a personal elaboration of data available in the market and from public sources.
- **BENCHMARK:** in the crude oil sector, a benchmark provides a reference parameter based on which other crudes are evaluated or priced. Some benchmarks are localized in specific geographic areas (e.g. Dubai in the Middle East or Tapis in the Asia-Pacific area) while others have global application, e.g. Brent Dated.
- **BLENDING of GASOLINES:** final operations in a refinery for mixing semi-finished products arriving from various plants. Actually, with very few exceptions, for technical/economic reasons, gasoline as a finished product is not directly obtained in a refinery from one sole plant, but usually through mixing various components.
- **DOWNSTREAM/UPSTREAM:** downstream is the part of the oil cycle that embraces transport, refining and marketing. The preceding operations, i.e. exploration and production of crude, represent the upstream.
- **DRIVING SEASON:** this term indicates the season for gasoline in America. Normally this phase starts in late May and continues for the entire summer season; in other words, as a result of summer travel, it is the period of greatest gasoline consumption in the USA.

- **ICE:** acronym for the Intercontinental Exchange, previously known as the International Petroleum Exchange (IPE), one of the major exchange markets for physical products and their derivates. The contracts dealt with on ICE include the following products: exchange rates, stocks and shares, crude and refined products, natural gas, coffee, cotton, sugar and so on. When reference is made to ICE futures, this signifies the futures contract for ICE Brent, dealt with in Europe on the London Exchange.
- **IEA:** Acronym for the International Energy Agency, an international organization founded by the Organization for Economic Cooperation and Development (OECD) with headquarters in Paris.
- **JET-FUEL** or **JET-KERO:** aviation fuel.
- **JOINT VENTURE:** a contract between organizations for the implementation of a project that involves notable technical and financial risks. The obligations and responsibilities of each partner are shared proportionately on the basis of each partner's participation quota in the project. Joint ventures between oil companies occur frequently in the exploration and exploitation of oilfields (in particular offshore ones).
- **OCTANE NUMBER:** the index of resistance to detonation of a fuel. If the octane number is too low the speed of combustion of the gasoline is too high and this causes shock waves in the combustion chamber of the engine ('pinking') and dispersion of energy.
- **NYMEX:** acronym for the New York Mercantile Exchange, one of the biggest commodity markets. Founded in 1872 for trading eggs, butter and cheese, it is now the reference bourse for oil. When the text refers to NYMEX futures this means the WTI futures contract.
- **OPEC:** acronym for the Organization of the Petroleum Exporting Countries.
- **OPEN INTEREST/OPEN POSITIONS**: in the futures market, this indicates the aggregate of the purchase and sale operations that have not been closed by operations in the opposite side.
- **TERMINAL OPERATOR:** the body that manages and administers a production terminal for crude oil (loading tankers, administration of production data, allocation of barrels). Normally this body coincides with the partner that has a majority shareholding in the project.
- **OSP:** Acronym for Official Selling Price. This provides one of the many ways for determining crude prices. The OSPs are normally fixed unilaterally and published by the producing countries.

- **SPARE CAPACITY:** in general, this refers to the unused capacity of a refinery (namely the capacity to produce greater quantities of refined products as compared with those already in production), or the unused production capacity of an oilfield (namely the capacity to produce greater quantities of crude oil as compared with those already in production).
- **SWING PRODUCER:** a producing country or association of such countries likely to adjust its offer of crude to the demand so as to control price movements.
- **ARMS-LENGTH TRANSACTIONS:** those between related parties but whose contractual terms reflect market conditions between independent and unrelated parties.
- **WTI:** acronym for West Texas Intermediate, also called Texas Light Sweet. This crude is used as a benchmark throughout America. The WTI derived contract is traded on the NYMEX.

List of Figures

List of Tables

List of Boxes

1
The World Crude Oil Paradoxes

For some years now, the price of oil has been out of control. None of the great names of the industry, the production cycle or the oil market is able to intervene to decide its level or guide its progress. The oil companies, the OPEC producing countries as well as the non-OPEC, the consuming countries, the consumers: not one of these has this capability.

The price of oil, in the imagination of western consumers, is still linked to the equilibrium developed during the 1970s and 1980s, with the emerging of the Persian Gulf countries and the OPEC nations.

It is still a popular belief that the cartel of the largest oil producing countries in the world is capable of regulating the volume of production and using this key raw material to achieve political aims.

Even today, when the price of oil rises beyond any level considered critical, the vast majority of the oil market analysts turn their eyes towards Vienna, where the oil ministers of the OPEC countries meet, imagining, hoping for and analysing decisions which either will not be taken or, if taken, will turn out to be completely ineffective. Lately, in some market reports, more sophisticated analyses are merely focused on the availability of OPEC countries' spare capacity; linking to this factor the dynamics of the oil price. When we look at the graph of the price of crude oil in Figure 1.1 we do not see the result of market forces, but rather a design traced by the hand of a powerful invisible architect who, following his own purposes, has established a course along which the price of oil should travel.

Since the end of 1998 analysts, oil companies and producing countries have mistaken every forecast of the price of oil, clearly showing not only that they no longer control the fundamental market mechanisms, but that they are not even able to comprehend its real dynamics – it is as if the invisible architect had lost his pencil.

If we take our memory back to December 1998, when the price of crude oil fell to $9 per barrel, all the respected names of the oil industry, bar none, forecast that the price would stay for at least one or two decades under $15 per barrel. It is enough to glance at the investment budgets of all the oil companies or the financial programmes of the producing

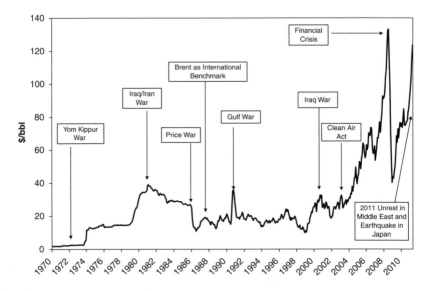

Figure 1.1   Brent Dated 1970–2010 and main historical events

countries to confirm that only the most optimistic among them estimated maximum price levels between $14 and $15 per barrel in the long run. Some oil companies, based on this view, hedged their production at this level of prices and went bankrupt. Yet only a few months later, in the summer of 2000, the price had already reached $35 per barrel, taking everyone – market analysts, oil companies, producing countries, economists, politicians and consumers – by surprise. Rivers of ink were consumed to explain the nature of this event through analysis where the causes were sought in transient factors; a sudden storm, nervousness between two OPEC countries, political uncertainties and so on.

The years of the energy crises were far away and deeply buried in the collective subconscious. The reappearance of such a thorny question was regarded, before it raised any anxiety, as almost a nuisance. Still today, after a decade of price hikes for crude from $9 to more than $140 and then down to $37 and once again above $120 per barrel, most people limit themselves to reciting a series of clichés to try to find justifications for an incomprehensible phenomenon:

- Limited supply from the producing countries, apparently inadequate to satisfy the growing demand for oil.
- Unexpected growth in the demand for oil by China and India, apparently upsetting the stability of the oil market.

- Tensions in the Middle East.
- The prospect of a decrease in the crude reserves/crude production ratio and therefore the availability of spare capacity.
- The excessive taxes on petroleum products (gasoline, diesel, LPG etc.) imposed by European governments.

This type of analysis has the advantage of being simple and easily presentable to the public at large, without, however, explaining what has really happened or is happening. Nevertheless, this approach has enabled some commentators to exaggerate on the contentious issues regarding the excessive power of the OPEC countries and the ways to bring them to reason.

The problem which all serious analysts have to face up to is actually quite simple. The essence is to explain oil price movements by use of the classic model of economics, which assumes that price is a function of the relationship between demand and supply:

$$Price = f\,(demand, supply)$$

This principle of economics seems too valid to allow any space for querying it. Notwithstanding this, the fundamental classic method applied *tout-court* to the oil market does not work. Yes, it is correct to say that the price is linked to the supply and demand balance, but of which good? We need to find out the merchandise or commodity whose supply and demand is determining the dynamics of oil price. For sure, it is not the physical crude oil.

OPEC has programmed and put into effect increases or cuts in production on numerous occasions, but always with scarce results. To every public announcement of increased production by the OPEC countries, the markets have responded with an increase in the crude oil price by at least a couple of dollars per barrel – and vice versa, when they announced cuts (Figure 1.2).

It is therefore reasonable to question whether the economic model utilized really works or if it is applied in an incorrect way to the oil market. Or, rather, that the technological complexity of this market does not allow it to be modelled on the simple relationship between demand and supply at a global level. The internal dynamics of this particular market require a much more detailed and complex model, capable of describing some of the fundamental dynamics of the system.

Unfortunately, the majority of analysts in this field have exclusively economic backgrounds and tend to apply general or econometric models to the crude oil, which are suitable for other commodities (coffee,

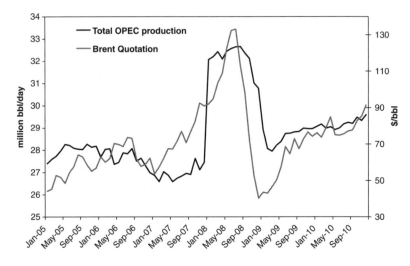

Figure 1.2 OPEC production versus Brent
Source: International Energy Agency

copper, gold etc.), where the production and technological transformation processes are less complex.

One starting point should be the recognition that what is commonly called the oil market is actually the conjunction and interaction of different markets which operate separately and independently but which are linked by certain complex forms of correlation and dynamics (Figure 1.3).

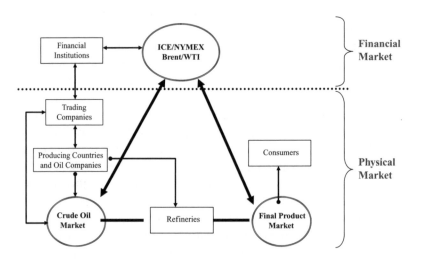

Figure 1.3 Complexity and interdependence in the oil market

We refer now to the crude oil market (raw material), to the finished products market (gasoline, diesel, jet fuel, fuel oil, chemical feedstocks, lubricants) and to the financial market for crude and finished products (futures). We should always remember that in our cars and in airplanes we do not use crude oil, but finished products, which are increasingly difficult to produce. We cannot also neglect the dramatic developments of the futures market and its predominant role in the world economy.

Each and all these markets respond to different behavioural patterns and they are operated by bodies with differing interests, culture and business objectives. A model that does not take into account the inter-relations between these markets and their individual dynamics is incapable of describing what happens to oil prices.

When the analyst is confronted by the unequivocal event of a price variation, and having only the classic model of the global demand/supply, he can only create a scenario of probable events (input to the model), which, when processed, might generate the variation in price which actually took place. If the price rises it is clear that there must have been an increase in demand or a reduction in supply. Therefore, one looks for all the clues which might prove that something like this has taken place. In the absence of reliable and prompt information there is more than enough space for these concoctions. It is thus very easy to reach the mistaken conclusion that China and India (the distant enemy, the invisible tartars) are becoming the critical factors for our planet. And that certainly OPEC (the conflict of civilizations) is yet again, for political and ideological reasons, not producing enough crude. Unquestionably there is no need to verify the production data of Venezuela under Chavez, or Iran under Ahmadinejad. It seems highly likely that both would wish to create problems for the west by raising prices.

The economic and strategic importance of the themes related to the price of crude oil would require a far more detailed technical analysis.

In this discussion we shall firstly try to examine the structural changes in the oil industry in recent decades, to see what has changed to make these dramatic and uncontrollable variations in price possible. And above all we shall try to understand why, in the space of a few short weeks (August–November 2008), without having seen even a small variation in the physical crude oil demand/supply situation the price tumbled from $144 to $37 per barrel. Then, in a couple of months it climbed back to $70–80 per barrel, exceeding again $120 per barrel in 2011. These events have silenced many analysts, who have not been able to provide consistent answers to the following questions. First of all, why did the price drop in 2008? What happened in those few weeks? Did the

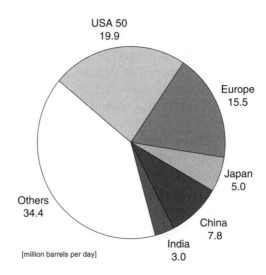

USA 50
19.9

Europe
15.5

Japan
5.0

China
7.8

India
3.0

Others
34.4

[million barrels per day]

Figure 1.4   World oil demand (average in 2005–2010), million barrels per day
Source: International Energy Agency

demands of China and India dry up or did the tensions in the Middle East calm down? Was OPEC flooding the markets with crude?

The truth is that OPEC cut production, the data regarding world demand for oil (see Figure 1.4) showed no reduction in global consumption, and – in the previous weeks – the Middle East lived through one of the most dramatic crises in recent history. In all this turmoil, the oil price plunged by almost $110 per barrel.

What is the factor that then pushed the price up again above $120 per barrel, during a worldwide dramatic economic crisis and stagnation of oil consumption?

Is there an economic model that can explain these recent events? A description will be attempted in the following pages.

2
The Market Events from 2008 to 2011

This conversation starts by taking a quick look at what happened in the international oil market during 2008. Actually, 2008 was the year when all the contradictions brewing in the previous decade surfaced. Events as dramatic as the collapse of crude oil to under $40 per barrel after a surge to more than $140 per barrel had never been seen before in the history of the oil industry. Not even the impressive crises of 1973 and 1979 were able to cause price swings of this size and speed.

It has already been mentioned that in the last decade, despite the available supply constantly exceeding the demand, we have witnessed the continual growth of the crude price.

The upward trend in prices underwent a brisk acceleration in spring 2008 and went on to touch a peak of $144 per barrel in summer (see Figure 2.1). After this we saw a spectacular nosedive of almost $110 per barrel. Analysts, economists and commentators have tried in all possible ways to provide explanations (sometimes far-fetched) for this phenomenon which apparently seemed unexplainable. In fact from the data available to all, we can safely say that in the passage from the phase of price increases to the phase of their fall, nothing changed in the physical oil market. On the contrary, in that very moment there was a seasonal increase in global demand of around 2 million barrels per day and a reduction in crude production of about the same amount. These changes should have worked in the opposite way, that is, an increasing price. The classic explanations (India, China, Middle East, crude oil reserves etc.) used by the analysts to explain the upward trend of the market became obsolete instantaneously and proved insufficient to account for the subsequent price tumble. The textbook explanations are unable to pinpoint the real causes behind everything.

Only recently some financial analysts have tried to link the fall of the price in November 2008 with the lack of financial capacity to open letters of credit of some traders, when trading their cargoes of oil. It is true that some banks had problems in issuing a letter of credit for

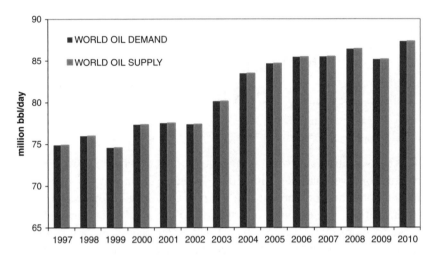

Figure 2.1 World oil demand versus supply

Source: International Energy Agency

some traders, but it was just a very marginal phenomenon relative only to very few cargoes in the market. The oil kept moving from the loading terminals to the end users, from the producers to the consumers. No interruption or excess of supply occurred at all and, therefore, nothing justified the fall of $110 per barrel.

It is not even comparable with the apparently similar events of 1986 and 1988 when the forward Brent market collapsed to $9 per barrel. At that time the oversupply of OPEC crude oil was real and the level of stocks evident.

WORLD ENERGY POLICY

It is important to clarify from the beginning that a short cut is not being sought by using a simplistic model where the financial speculation is soley responsible for all the chaos in the oil market. The financial investments are likely just taking advantage of the existing paradoxes and bottlenecks in the oil industry and in the energy policy worldwide. The stability will eventually come only when and if these structural problems are solved.

For the time being we are just observing further additional elements of crisis arriving and making the scenario even worse. The North Africa crisis (Libya in particular) and the Fukushima nuclear accident are referred to.

These two events will amplify the structural crisis of the oil market, accelerating all the processes already in progress since the Chernobyl accident.

We have already experienced in all the industrialized countries the lack of an energy policy that is capable of harmonizing the growing energy demand with the new respect for the environment. The development of environmental regulations in the last two decades has created burdensome (but unchallengeable) limits for the energy and oil companies in particular, but has not driven the bodies concerned to make the investments necessary to create 'compliant' energy and products. The result of these divergent processes has been the net reduction of availability of finished products marketable in the western industrialized countries. There is now a shortage of clean gasoline and gasoil. In total the shortfall in the USA amounts to about 50 million tonnes per year of gasoline, and about 40 million tonnes per year of gasoil in Europe. To bridge these gaps it is necessary to import from other geographical areas, which obviously deprives local consumers of these products or forces them to pay the higher prices that consumers in the strong countries can pay to get their hands on the missing products. It is a real competition where the winners are always the ones who can pay more.

A glance at the newspapers is enough to discover the limitations imposed on motorists in Middle Eastern countries (Iran, Egypt etc.) or all of West Africa.

The deficit of these high-quality finished products has bolstered the rise in crude oil prices, particularly the light varieties such as those from the North Sea or North Africa. Somewhat similar to what would happen if, for some strange reason, a rule were introduced to allow the sale of only choice cuts of meat (fillet steak, entrecôte, silverside): the price of these would rise but so would the price of the cow.

This potential shortage of finished products has spread the feeling in the trading market that something is at risk and, on a daily basis, somebody may not be able to get the product he or she is looking for. The oil market has become nervous and very transient, with the same level of volatility experienced during the Gulf wars (when the risk of a shortage of supply was evident).

The recent dramatic events (Fukushima and Libya) will definitely amplify the already existing concerns and tensions and will spread the sensitivity about the environmental issues worldwide and accelerate the increase of the demand for clean products.

We cannot forget that the only decision taken at the global political level in one of the G20 meetings, to reduce the impact on the economy of the increasing price of oil, was to encourage the construction of new nuclear plants for producing electricity. This decision was inadequate already when it was taken (less than 10% of the oil is used to produce electricity) but today, after Fukushima, it appears to be almost obsolete. We can say without any doubt that there is a lack of energy policy worldwide, but especially in the industrialized countries; only China and India are building what they need, despite the apparent general market indication.

The world oil market is already in the middle of these tensions, but we have not yet seen the worst. The forthcoming summers will offer some anticipation of the future developments we can expect in the near future, with a shortage of supply of high-quality gasoline and clean gasoil and a significant increase of the price differential between light and heavy crude oils.

Later the combined impact of the reduction of the sweet light crude oils (like the ones produced by Libya) and the shortage of clean products will be examined with more technical detail and analysis. An understanding will be gained as to why Saudi Arabia was ready to increase the production to compensate the reduction of supply from Libya, but, after a couple of weeks had to stop producing additional barrels of oil.

The quality (more than the quantity) of the crude oils offered to the market is today a crucial factor for meeting the demand of products worldwide. With the existing quality of the raw materials, it takes new technologies and massive investments in the refinery industry. We are far away from implementing such solutions worldwide.

It is evident that the structural problems for the oil industry will remain as they are in the next decade and they will keep providing grounds for financial speculation and therefore for the increase of prices, as has happened in the last ten years.

THE FINANCIAL CRISIS AND THE OIL MARKET

In December 1988, OPEC decided to adopt as reference for the price of crude oil (rather than the value of the Arabian light, the Saudi crude of light quality) the value of the Brent.

At that time, everyone thought that this was the value of the crude produced in the North Sea, the name of which was indeed Brent. No-one realized that this was a misunderstanding, a case of a homonym. The Brent in question was not a crude oil, but a financial commodity.

Let us imagine, for a moment and as a game, which OPEC had decided to adopt, as a reference for fixing the price of oil, the value of a particular type of cherry tomato, to which the creator and biggest producer gave the name of 'Brent'. The reason for the choice could have been the high energy consumption needed to produce the new 'Brent' cherry tomato.

Once the decision was taken, it would become obvious that the price of oil would depend, almost exclusively, on the supply and demand of Brent tomatoes on the international market. A plentiful harvest would equal low prices and a difficult year, high prices. Cherry tomatoes in fashion means high prices; and so on.

No-one would dream of looking, to analyse the movements of the price or to make predictions of the future, at the supply and demand of the physical crude oil.

We have taken the above example as a joke, but one capable, although with the differentiation needed and analyses concerned, of giving us a description that is fairly close to reality. These dynamics of the oil market are slowly beginning to become clear and understandable to the principal subjects in the oil market, producing countries and oil companies.

What is in fact the Brent market, the true one that defines the price of oil?

This is a huge game like the 'Panini football stickers', those carrying the picture of football players. The stickers, once printed and sold, create an exchange market between the children or fans that look for them, and their value varies according to the demand. Those of the famous and popular players will go for more than those of unknown or less well-known players.

Let us imagine that one day, for some reason, the football teams of the world, with the agreement of UEFA and FIFA, decide that the market value of the various players is that of the respective stickers or that they are indexed to that reference.

A double market would be created, that of the football market where against real money a club recruits a player in flesh and blood, and the other where everyone can buy or sell stickers without ever becoming owners of a player. If the market of the stickers should develop massively, thanks to the ease with which it is possible to buy and sell (online for example), it could at a certain point become a form of investment in itself, with participants that have never been interested in football and even less in stickers.

If an international bank, for various reasons, should invest significant amounts of capital in the stickers of a particular player, this would cause an increase in value, regardless of the performance of the player and the policy of the club to which the player belongs.

We would say that the football market has slipped through the hands of the operators of that sport and has become an instrument of financial speculation with positive and negative effects also for the world of football (profits or losses for the bodies that 'own' the players whose stickers are the subject of speculation).

Something similar has taken place in the world of oil. In the eighties a sticker market was created, that of the futures contracts, which is just like plastic cards (or stickers) on which a barrel of crude is depicted. Whoever buys these plastic cards buys the drawing of a barrel, but does not have any possibility of exchanging a plastic card with a real barrel. The market of the oil stickers is a market that is almost totally independent from the real oil market, with bodies operating there and dominating it (controlling it and manipulating it) that normally have no relationship with or interest in the oil industry.

In December 1988, the OPEC countries decided that the price of their crude oils would be fixed on the basis of the value of the 'oil stickers'. This was an almost unnoticed change of a geo-political nature that transferred control and management of the international oil market out of the hands of the OPEC countries into those of the City of London and, slightly less so, Wall Street. This was the event that overturned the balance of the power that had been established since the crisis of 1973.

For years the constant expansion of this parallel market supported the real market. The value of the 'drawing of the barrel' was almost always higher than the one the physical market would have guaranteed, bringing benefits to those who invest in this sector and to the various producing countries. Yes, it is a crazy game, but with a useful purpose.

In the autumn of 2008, the bankruptcy of the principal banks, which owned massive quantities of oil stickers, obliged them to sell the oil stickers and therefore cause a slump in the value of such stickers and hence in the price of oil, the reference value of which derives from these.

From that moment there began talks about the need to review the mechanism used to set the price of oil, but quietly and without haste.

During 2009, the oil price, thanks to the recovery of what we called the sticker market (where the banks have placed a significant share of the money received from the governments), started to increase again.

The attitude of the producing countries became: let us discuss, examine and wait. Any action will eventually be taken if and when the banks find more profitable ways to invest their money, not in the Panini stickers anymore but maybe in the real economy. For now, we carry on this way.

So we have to resign ourselves to seeing the price of oil go up and down, avoiding having to pretend to be able to explain the correlations between these fluctuations and the fundamentals of the oil industry or the non-existing policies of OPEC.

For most of 2009 and 2010, we saw the price fluctuating, in the range of $70–80 per barrel. Everybody started to announce the new kind of ideal range of the price of oil, considered sacred by the main OPEC official representatives. As usual the market, a few months later, deviated from all these guidelines given by the gurus and by the authorities. We can say, then, that since December 1988 the global reference for the price of crude has lost its direct relationship with the physical market.

Initially, the oil futures market had in common with the oil market, apart from the name Brent, the historic fact that it was born to support the trading operations of the oil companies, as a financial instrument to provide risk hedging against oscillations in crude oil prices.

At the start of the year 2000, the oil futures market detached itself almost completely from its original nature, becoming a market purely for financial purposes. International banks entered this business without having any involment in the oil business, just as an opportunity to make profit, but some oil companies and almost all the oil trading organizations also started to consider the futures market as an independent business beyond the hedging purposes. All those analysts who tried to explain the movements of the crude oil price on the basis of the evolution of the relationship between demand and supply of physical crude have failed, simply because the link between the financial market and the crude oil market has become increasing ephemeral or even non-existent.

The graph in Figure 2.2 clearly shows how the volume of business on the crude oil futures market has risen tenfold in the last 10 years, closely following the entry of the great financial institutions in this field and the change in the attitude of the traditional oil players. This has caused the complete disruption of the internal dynamics of the oil market.

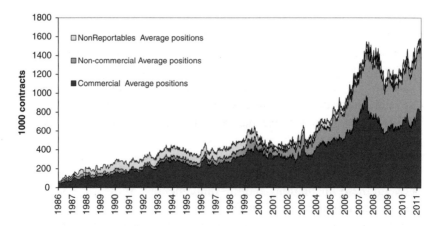

Figure 2.2 NYMEX WTI crude oil futures open interest: non-commercial versus total traders

Source: NYMEX

Brent (on paper, financial) is now traded on the market simply for investment purposes or financial speculation, to protect capital by parking it in a safe place for a certain period of time (even just for a few minutes), to profit from a momentary wave of speculation, or to manipulate a market which otherwise would be stable.

To understand better the size of the phenomenon, let us glance at the numbers of this business (see Figure 2.3), which is almost unknown to those who complain about the price of gasoline.

During 2008–2010, with world crude production around 86 million barrels per day, only about 20 million barrels per day were marketed. The remainder, about 65 million barrels per day, was not put on the international markets because it was consumed directly by the producing countries.

If we refer to a valuation made in the period January 2008–December 2010, with an average price for Brent of $80 per barrel, we can easily calculate that the value of the mass of money in movement due to purchases and sales of physical crude as traded amounts to around $1,900 billion. If we further assume that all the crude produced (86 million barrels per day) was traded at market price, the mass of money in play, in the same period from January 2008 to December 2010, would have been around $7,600 billion. The balance between demand and supply of physical crude at world level fluctuates within these values.

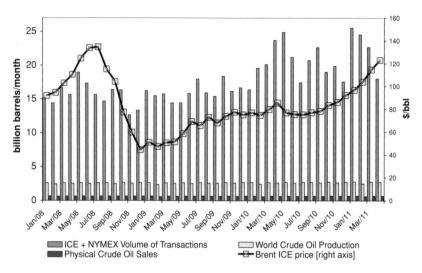

Figure 2.3 Comparison between volumes of NYMEX and Brent traded in the futures and physical markets

Sources: NYMEX and International Energy Agency

Now we can look at the volumes traded on the Exchange to discover that we have a totally different picture and with degrees of magnitude enormously higher. During 2008–2010, about $51,000 billion were traded on the futures market, that is to say, 27 times more than the value traded on the physical market and about six to seven times more than the entire world production of crude.

Table 2.1 shows a situation with daily trades of about $46 billion (about $4 billion per working hour), just as if on the crude market about 580 million barrels per day were traded on the crude market and not the 20 million actually commercialized or the 86 produced. What are these 580 million barrels per day on paper, which have nothing to do with the oil market and the demand and supply of oil for energy consumption, and what influence do they have on the pricing system for petroleum products? What effect do they have on the price of gasoline for the poor motorist?

In theory the futures market for Brent was created to stabilize crude prices after the epic oil crises of the 1970s and 1980s. The daily quotation for Brent was supposed to permit greater transparency in the transactions and thus a stabilization of prices in the short and medium term. In the early years this was the case; the volumes of crude traded on the futures

Table 2.1 Comparative analysis of the value of NYMEX and Brent in the financial and physical markets

	January 2008–December 2010				
	Production of Physical Crude Oil	Transactions of Physical Crude Oil	Transaction of equivalent oil in the financial market	Ratio Futures/ Physical	Ratio Physical/ Futures
Volume					
(billion barrels)	93.7	23.4	623.1	27	3.8%
Value (billion $)	7,594	1,899	50,806	27	3.7%

Sources: NYMEX and International Energy Agency

market never exceeded the physical quantities produced and sold. This can only mean that the oil companies operated on the paper market to stabilize the price of their crudes with hedging operations. Today we see 580 million barrels of oil equivalent arriving on the market – which strangely enough we continue to call an oil market – and they are behind the real dynamics that move the quotation for Brent, which is still called, for no good reason, the price of crude oil.

Let us give an even more concrete example. At the end of June 2008 the price of Brent touched levels above $140 per barrel. Rivers of ink flowed to try to explain the reasons behind this increase. There was discussion of the threats from China and India, the fall in world oil reserves, geopolitical scenarios, stock variances and so on. But a simple, crude and dramatic truth was overlooked. The level of prices above the $140 per barrel number, which in June was used to trade the commodity called oil, does not derive from the market for this particular commodity and is not the result of the demand and supply balance of this merchandise. It has nothing to do with oil. Going back to our previous example, the crisis was in the cherry tomato (called Brent) market, not in the market of the crude oil (called also Brent).

Thus, to try to explain its dynamics using models related to the market for consumption and production of energy will be an exercise carried out in vain.

During the whole month of June, about 700 million barrels of crude (the physical kind that dirties your hands if you touch it) were traded. In the same month on the paper market for Brent up to 20,000 million equivalent barrels were traded, in other words nearly 30 times more than the physical market.

In the course of 2008, just when the wind seemed to be blowing the prices towards $144 per barrel, the long-awaited event took place, namely the crash of the banks and the main international financial institutions, which also burst the oil bubble. Following the bankruptcy of some banks and the much-reduced liquidity of many financial institutions, transactions in the Petroleum Exchange quickly nosedived, at the same time bringing down the price of Brent to under $40 per barrel.

In this context OPEC, aware of a dramatic curtailment in the revenues of various member countries, tried to keep up appearances and show a minimum level of action, announcing and trying to implement cuts in production to bolster up the crude price which was in free-fall (from the $144 per barrel of July to the $40 per barrel of December). Such a collapse had never been seen in the history of the oil industry. As usual, the result of the cuts announced was the continuation of the fall in prices, confirming the completely insignificant influence of OPEC on the dynamics of crude oil prices.

From the data we have seen, it follows that *OPEC represents 30% of a segment of 4% of the business that we call the oil market*. This being so, how can it have a significant influence on price trends?

The great financial crisis has, however, highlighted some important novelties in the international oil market scenario. In the year 2008, we saw the downturn in the financial activity on the futures market (see Figure 2.4). Daily trades of oil contracts on the financial markets fell from levels of almost $282 billion per day in June to around $75 billion per day at year-end: a nosedive of almost 4 times.

Fundamentals or financial speculation?

During the second part of 2008 the exclusively financial activities of the banks disappeared progressively from the crude oil futures market, leaving mainly the oil companies and the physical market professionals to operate for the sole purpose of covering the risk of price fluctuations: in other words, we digressed back to a market structure closer to that of the late 1990s. The players of the oil market, although for a very limited period of time, were once again the physical producers, oil producers and oil companies. The price of crude, although still linked to the movements of the crude markets of London and New York, during the last quarter of 2008 and the first one of 2009 seemed more closely correlated to the balance of demand and supply in the physical market,

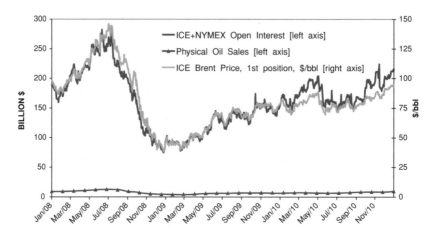

Figure 2.4   Futures: daily trades in 2008–2010
Source: NYMEX

moving in the range of $40–50 per barrel, which, at that time, seemed
to represent a reasonable and long-lasting point of balance.

Box 2.1   Cost of the Marginal Barrel

The crisis of November 2008 confirmed an important indication about
what price level crude oil would have reached if driven exclusively by
physical balances in the demand and supply of gasoline and gasoil.
Everyone remembers that until the 1990s, whenever there was a crisis
of excess supply in the market, the crude price quickly fell below $10
per barrel. This price represented the production cost in the marginal
fields at that time, namely offshore wells in the North Sea or the
Texas Gulf.

Holding the price at those levels removed the production of part
of such crudes from the market and thus contributed to realigning
supply and demand, or at least it triggered actions on the international
market (or international political decisions), which created stability.

Today the marginal fields are the producing wells borderline from
the technological point of view, such as the tar sands of Canada or
Venezuela, or certain offshore fields in ultra deep waters.

Production costs in these fields are over $40 per barrel. This is,
therefore, the new lower limit to the crude price. Below this there
would be a drastic stoppage in the flow of energy to fundamental

areas of the industrialized countries, with severe consequences for the economy.

Table 2.2   Total production costs by region

Region	2003–2005 $/boe	2004–2006 $/boe	Delta %
USA			
Onshore	14.00	19.46	39
Offshore	50.56	69.75	38
Total USA	16.70	23.16	39
Canada	23.84	26.59	12
Europe	16.43	29.79	81
Africa	22.26	32.13	44
Middle East	9.78	14.31	46
Others			
Eastern Hemisphere	14.98	18.76	25
Western Hemisphere	31.06	47.63	53
Worldwide	**17.45**	**24.29**	**39**

Source: International Energy Agency

We therefore have always suggested abandoning scenarios which contemplate further falls in price down to the levels of the past and to be realistic with regard to the possibility of increases in the near future.

During 2009, as it is well known, all the major international banks, which were saved by the governments, re-started to invest the money received again in the financial market and in particular in the oil futures (back to the stickers market). The result has been the increase of the price of oil during the period of lower consumption. Then, at the end of 2010 the price of crude reached a level of $90 per barrel with an average of $10 per barrel above the value of 2009, and in 2011 (the time of writing) is already above $120 per barrel. The imaginary new equilibrium value, established in the range of $70–80 per barrel, does not exist anymore. It has just gone. This increase of about $50 per barrel in two years, above the ideal range, was once again beyond any expectations.

The recent events, after 2009, in the oil market have reopened the discussion about the real reason for the price uptrend. Many analysts have concluded that the new trend is firmly supported by strong fundamentals and the financial 'investments' are just following suit.

Despite some positive signs in the evolution of the oil demand, we do not think that what has happened in the last three years and the recent increase of the oil price can be explained simply through the evolution of the fundamentals.

The analysis of the dynamics of the market has currently become complex and the distinction between the effects due to the pure financial activity (speculation) or due to the fundamentals is not so clear.

First of all, we should try to take into account the deep change in the organization and in the attitude of the financial institutions playing in the oil futures market.

The financial institutions in the last few years have invested in hiring experts and traders from the physical oil markets. They normally don't move a drop of oil, but they plan their financial operations following closely the evolution of the fundamentals and every single rumour about the life of the oil industry. They move their money based on these elements of information. We have already seen the dimension of the impact of the movement of this amount of money, which is so massive to overcome the 'natural' dynamics of the physical market. There are always overreactions due to the enormous flow of money and number of transactions on the futures market. What in the past would have caused a price fluctuation of a few cents per barrel, nowadays can produce a price change of many dollars per barrel.

Sometimes the direction of the financial operations are in line with the fundamentals, but there are moments where the money is moved to or from the oil futures market because of the evolution of other commodities and with no relationship at all to the dynamics of the oil world. It looks like the new alignments between finance and fundamentals materialize in the mind of financial traders.

In Figure 2.5 we can see how fragile is the link between the fundamentals and the price of oil, taking also into account that the actual data of the supply and demand become available (and reliable) with delays of months, when the price is already history.

Of course, the financial analysts are very proud to affirm that all the financial investments are made only on the basis of the oil market fundamentals. And the investors seem to trust them.

It seems, however, evident that the real alignment between the fundamentals and the financial activity takes place in the minds of the financial traders.

For this reason it is useful to have a look at the real physical market since the financial crisis also became an economic crisis. Let's have a

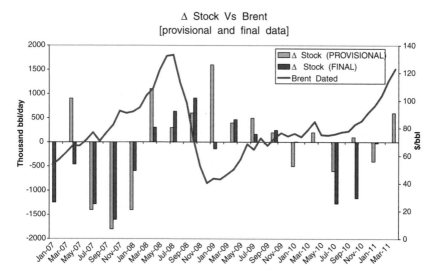

Figure 2.5   Provisional and final assessments of stock changes versus Brent prices
Source: International Energy Agency

look at some relevant phenomena which have affected the evolution of the prices, and let's try to understand better the role of the financial speculation.

DEMAND/SUPPLY OF GASOLINE AND GASOIL

Looking at the actual data, in Table 2.3, about oil consumption in Europe and the USA, it is evident that we are still facing a downward trend in oil consumptions in the main western consuming countries, with some substantial differences between Europe and the USA. During 2010 we still had a declining trend in Europe, but a quite positive reaction in the USA.

However, the main element of the analysis is not the direction of the global consumption in these main market areas, but the evolution of some critical products.

When the Brent price was at its peak, some signs of the economic crisis started to show up and all the analysts were looking for a possible fall in US gasoline demand, a fall considered responsible for triggering a sort of domino effect inside the world oil market (crash in the demand

Table 2.3 Demand of oil products in OECD Europe and in the USA

OECD Europe [kbbl/day]	2007	2008	2009	2010	2011	Δ 2008–2007	Δ 2009–2008	Δ 2010–2009
LPG and Ethane	993	1,016	924	924	921	23	−92	0
Naphtha	1,283	1,157	1,108	1,208	1,220	−126	−49	100
Motor Gasoline	2,481	2,360	2,287	2,195	2,128	−121	−73	−92
Jet and Kerosene	1,303	1,323	1,267	1,270	1,297	20	−56	3
Gas/Diesel Oil	6,117	6,269	6,021	6,138	6,155	152	−248	117
Diesel	4,273	4,290	4,228	4,334	4,416	17	−62	106
Other Gasoils	1,844	1,979	1,793	1,804	1,739	135	−186	11
Residual Fuels	1,725	1,661	1,434	1,290	1,214	−64	−227	−144
Other Products	1,552	1,572	1,451	1,405	1,451	20	−121	−46
Total Products	15,453	15,357	14,493	14,431	14,387	−96	−864	−62

United States [kbbl/day]	2007	2008	2009	2010	2011	Δ 2008–2007	Δ 2009–2008	Δ 2010–2009
LPG and Ethane	2,091	1,959	2,056	2,113	2,104	−132	97	57
Naphtha	294	248	246	263	241	−46	−2	17
Motor Gasoline	9,355	9,047	9,055	9,129	9,169	−308	8	74
Jet and Kerosene	1,696	1,587	1,446	1,493	1,526	−109	−141	47
Gas/Diesel Oil	4,277	4,013	3,700	3,852	3,889	−264	−313	152
Diesel	3,520	3,484	3,221	3,345	3,401	−36	−263	124
Other Gasoils	757	529	478	507	489	−228	−51	29
Residual Fuels	818	702	591	642	610	−116	−111	51
Other Products	2,498	2,233	1,971	2,059	2,068	−265	−262	88
Total Products	21,028	19,789	19,065	19,551	19,606	−1,239	−724	486

Source: International Energy Agency

for US gasoline, interruption of gasoline imports from Europe, fall in prices in Europe and, thus, a nosedive in crude prices).

Now we know that the real market evolution was quite different. Actually, the crude price did fall to around $40 per barrel but the gasoline demand in the USA did not vary significantly. In fact, in the course of 2008 there was a reduction of only 3% in gasoline consumption, far below the level required to significantly reduce the flow of high-octane components imported from Europe and South America. After this slowdown of the demand in 2008 the gasoline consumption already gradually started to rise again in 2009.

There is a structural element in the USA market, too often overlooked by many analysts, which can keep the price of gasoline at a very high level, despite any weakness on the demand side.

As we will examine later in detail, the US environmental legislation has churned out some monstrosities, such as the possibility for each State to request gasoline specifications differing from the national standards. About 40 different types of gasoline are thus on sale, distributed in the various States and counties of the nation, creating immense difficulties for the productive system to face. Each marketer is forced to import, or swap with other refiners in neighbouring States, the components for blending gasolines (as we will examine later, gasoline is not a product but a mixture of products and semi-finished products which together guarantee certain characteristics: octane number, density, a limited presence of aromatics, olephines etc.) to formulate a product which is marketable in the particular area.

As of today, the volume of high-octane components imported into the USA remains close to 1 million barrels per day, keeping a certain level of tension in the international market, which serves to prop up the crude prices (remember the example of the price of fillet steak and the cow).

The decrease of the demand was more drastic in Europe both in terms of gasoline and gasoil, but, because of the flow of the export of gasoline to the traditional USA market and to other new destinations (Middle East, West Africa), there was not a dramatic impact on the price system.

This structural strength of the fundamentals, once again, has given a new progressive confidence to the financial operators that the oil business was still worth investing in and was still the most reliable and liquid market among all the other commodities.

A similar phenomenon happened for the gasoil market, where the decline of the demand has been balanced by the introduction of more severe quality specifications in the European market (January 2008).

WTI – BRENT DIFFERENTIAL

A further example of how the financial speculation can thrive on the basis of some structural constraints of the oil industry is useful here. Brent and WTI are the two main crude oils used in the futures market: Brent in London (ICE) and WTI in New York (NYMEX). WTI is a crude of better quality than Brent and its price has always been higher, in the range of $1–4 per barrel. In the last years, we have seen the price of WTI being lower than Brent by up to $18 less per barrel.

Looking at all the crude oils of the worse quality, none of them is priced with such a discount to Brent. This unbelievable event has engaged all the analysts in a debate. Analyses and interpretations have been given, trying to link the dynamics of the prices with the fundamentals of the US market.

Of course, it is very hard to explain why a bottle of high-quality champagne should be sold at the price of a low-quality carton of red wine.

Box 2.2   Jet Fuel and Gasoil Market

The only sector that was really hit by the crisis was that of aviation. The consumption of jet fuel in the USA fell by over 10% and was accompanied by cuts in the flights of all the main airlines (Continental reduced its flights by almost 15%). These were the only data that measured a change of habits in the USA, in both the business and the private worlds. Obviously, since this is a variation in a limited segment of US oil demand (jet fuel represents less than 10% of the total demand), it is not a key factor in determining a change in the crude price levels. The reduction of jet fuel consumption, however, had an impact in the evolution of the winter gasoil market. In fact, kerosene (from which jet fuel is obtained) is also used for mixing with gasoil to improve its quality.

Both the USA and Europe need to import huge quantities of gasoil during the winter season. The countries that can supply gasoil in excess, in relation to their own domestic consumption, are Russia and the Persian Gulf nations. Unfortunately the quality of the products from these sources is not in line with the environmental specifications in the west (excessive sulphur contents) and they, therefore, have to be processed in refinery desulphurization plants or blended with semi-finished products of higher quality. Kerosene is one of these.

This was the key element that affected price movements during the winter months of 2008–2009: the supply capacity of the western refining system for clean, high-quality gasoil (see Figure 2.6). If the winter had been mild, as it was in the 2006–2007 season, the demand of heating gasoil would have been limited and the production would have been easily capable of supplying the system without putting any pressure on the prices.

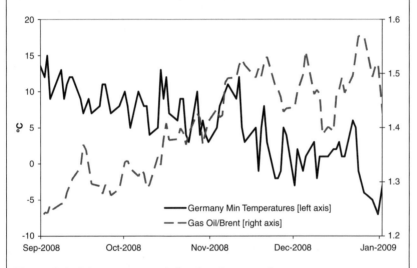

Figure 2.6 Price movements during the winter months

The fact that the winter was colder than any in the previous decade, once again showed the bottlenecks in the production system, just as they did in the past, which had powerful effects on both the gasoil and the crude oil price, giving ground and confidence to the financial investors putting their money in the oil futures market again. From November 2008 until March 2009, the thermometer decided the crude oil price in the major areas of consumption (USA, Europe). All the other factors (OPEC policy, macro-economic and geopolitical scenarios etc.) continued to act purely as aesthetic embellishments to the scenario.

This is a typical example where, unless we take into consideration the combined action of the financial speculation with the industry constraints, we are not be able to understand the dynamic of that anomalous event.

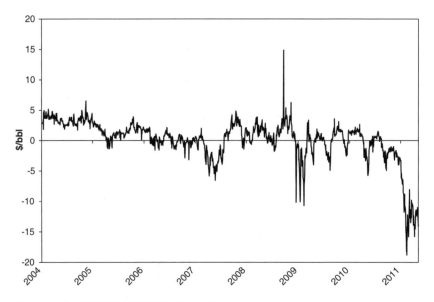

Figure 2.7   WTI NYMEX–ICE Brent differential
Source: NYMEX

All the crude oils produced in the south of the USA are collected in Cushing, Oklahoma and then sent, via pipelines, to the north. All the pipelines have one direction, south to north. The opposite direction has never been considered, because it would have been meaningless. However, it is a matter of fact that it is not possible to move the WTI from Cushing to the refineries on the east coast of the USA. Based on this fact, the financial investors started to sell WTI on NYMEX and buy Brent on ICE, inverting and widening the price spread between the two crude oils, with WTI becoming cheaper and cheaper (see Figure 2.7).

In order to re-balance the market anomaly it would have been necessary to move WTI to the east coast, where the price of Brent was $18 per barrel higher, but, as we have seen, there are no pipelines able to transport the crude in that direction. In other words, we are in the situation where the market is unable to guarantee any feedback to create the condition for the re-adjustment of the previous equilibrium. It has become impossible to limit the action of the financial speculation.

Actually, one of the investors in this specific business, hired all the railways capacity from Cushing to the Atlantic coast, in advance and started to transport some WTI, making a lot of profit on the spread artificially created. Just to prove that the event was planned in the financial environment many months in advance. Once again, the financial speculation (or financial investment) operates and thrives on the existing industry constraints and structural problems of the market. Very often this massive activity doesn't allow the market to activate the physiological feedbacks to overcome or accelerate the solution of the problems, which become heavier and therefore encourage an increasing level of speculation.

It is instructive to observe the graph in Figure 2.8, which shows the movement of the volatility of the price of Brent from 1988 to 2011. To simplify, the volatility has been defined as the difference between the highest and lowest value recorded during the same month. One can see clearly that historically the volatility index of the crude price remained between $1 and $2 per barrel until the end of the 1990s. The only exception was seen in 1981 at the time of the first Gulf War when the volatility index touched $15 per barrel. These dramatic changes in price evidently reflected the uncertainty in the market and the continual changes in the expectations of the trading world. Starting from the early 2000s, we note that volatility indices over $10 per barrel became a constant feature in the market, even in the absence of factors engendering tension in the market comparable to those of times of war in the Persian Gulf area; as if we were continuously facing a situation of potential short supply. This graph also tells us that there is a date in the evolution

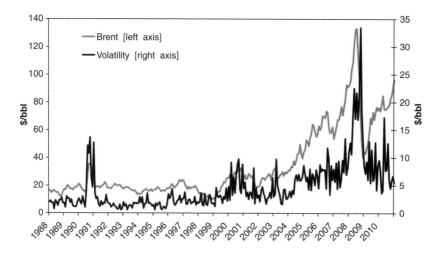

Figure 2.8 Brent and inter-monthly volatility (1988–2011)

of the dynamics of the oil market after which the break with the past takes shape. We believe that a study of the evolution of the price of crude oil must start out from this observation and try to understand what happened at the beginning of the year 2000.

The economic crisis may have appeared, in some moments, to have lessened the impact of the structural bottlenecks of the oil industry but certainly not to have removed them. The North Africa crisis and the Fukushima nuclear accident are here to remind us that there is a structural energy crisis that we shall have to face up to and how large the lack of awareness is in the political leadership of the main industrialized countries.

In the following pages we shall try to reconstruct the processes which have led to the growing divergence between the physical crude oil market and the dynamics of the crude oil price. In particular we shall consider:

- The effects deriving from certain historical decisions by the OPEC producing countries, such as the indexing of the price of their crudes to the financial market of Brent crude.
- The distortions created by the new environmental laws, in the context of the lack of adequate investments in the world refining sector.

These phenomena could have been described in a different order. However, this one was chosen for its ability to enable the reader to follow, in a more linear way, the creation of the puzzle, even if the tie-up between the various aspects is such that only in the end the overall reasoning will become intelligible, together with the model with which today the evolution of the oil market can be interpreted.

3

Evolution of the Price of Crude Oil from the 1960s up to 1999

The structural characteristics of the oil industry that have supported the rising trend of prices in the past decade have already been mentioned. They do not explain, however, why the world of finance has managed to grasp almost complete control of this oil market and the system that fixes the price of crude, pushing aside producing countries as well as the oil companies. The process and the mechanisms that have made this transformation possible will be examined. For this purpose and against this background we have to revisit the main events in oil history in the last decades and particularly the suicidal decisions of the OPEC countries, as well as to analyse the technical mechanisms in the Brent market (forward and its futures).

Obviously it is not the author's intention to describe the history of oil, already told in detail by many prestigious writers, but only to provide a way of looking at the events just as a plain professional in this field would have done, living through them and interpreting them, but to whom the descriptions made by others did not seem convincing and coherent with what he or she observed day by day in the market. Avoidance is intentional of a purely political view of the various events – for which valuable studies and analyses exist – by limiting ourselves to the search for the appropriate economic model within which the oil market has moved, in its different historic situations.

The aim is to understand whether prices have evolved in an oligopoly or in a free market situation. And in this latter case, what has kept it at price levels higher than the laws of the market would seem to permit?

In particular, the aim is to be able to reply to the question that was put forth at the start of this story and which comes to mind spontaneously when we look at Figure 3.1 showing the historical evolution of the price of crude: is the curve which traces the movements in price a sequence of values that mark *a posteriori* the free dynamics of the market, namely the result of the interaction between demand and supply, or is it the design that an invisible hand has traced day after day for decades?

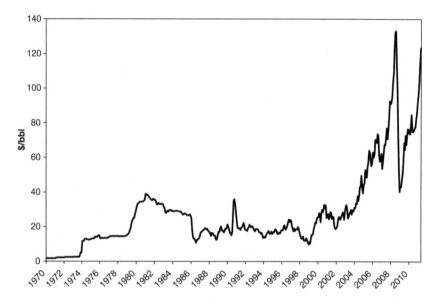

Figure 3.1   Crude oil prices (1970–2011)

1960–1980: THE OIL MONOPOLY AND THE TWO CRISES IN THE 1970s

We could start our tale by saying: 'once upon a time there was the price of crude oil'. Actually, the price of crude oil has existed for many years and it was the amount of money with which one could purchase a physical cargo of crude to put on a ship and take it to a refinery to transform it into gasoline, gasoil and other products. Today, however, when we speak of the price of Brent, it is not clear what we are talking about; above all it is not clear what we can buy with that amount of money. But let us take things in order.

In the 1960s and up to 1973, the price of crude was a number, more or less fixed, established unilaterally by the big US oil companies, who had a monopoly in the market. The experts in the energy sectors in charge of forecasting the price of crude oil for the current year used to describe the model employed for the forecast with the following, colourful but effective, phrase: 'take the price used by Exxon, add it to that used by Shell and divide the sum by two'. Until 1973, there was no way to mistake the price forecast, it was just a simple average. The price that was officially fixed and published was one alone, that of the benchmark (reference price), namely Arabian Light crude, the main

Figure 3.2   The price of crude with reference to the benchmark

crude of medium–high-quality produced in Saudi Arabia. The prices of all the other crudes were established by referring to the benchmark and fixing a price differential that took account of their price, quality and marketability (see Figure 3.2).

This was a classic situation of monopoly/oligopoly, featuring perfect control of the supply by the producers. The prices were completely stable, since the producers were able to regulate supply according to any fluctuation in demand.

OPEC (Organization of Petroleum Exporting Countries) was formed in 1960, with the main objective being to create some form of control in the oil market by establishing co-ordination between the various countries regarding the structure of the mineral contracts. However, control of the price of crude remained firmly in the hands of the multinational companies until 1973. In fact, only the majors were able to control the production of crude together with the flow of purchases by the refineries (almost all of them owned by the same companies).

In 1973, with the Yom Kippur war, we witnessed the first historic overturn in the world oil market. The Arab countries, following the Israeli–Palestine conflict, declared an oil embargo on those countries that supported Israel, particularly the USA and Holland. OPEC took control of crude prices and started to publish a price list each year, always based on Arabian Light as the benchmark. Saudi Arabia, being the principal producing country, but above all being the producer of the benchmark, took on the leadership of OPEC. From that moment it became the task of Saudi Arabia to fine-tune the supply of Arabian Light on the market to stabilize its price around the value published by OPEC.

Under the control of the OPEC countries, and thanks to the scare sparked off by the Middle East crisis, the crude price rose from the $2 per barrel level to $12–15 per barrel. This was the first great oil crisis that citizens of the main consuming countries witnessed; going on foot or by bicycle during their weekends and holidays. It was in this extremely emotional context, characterized by a strong sense of participation and awareness, that debate was opened concerning the need for diversification of energy sources; massive investment programmes were tabled for the construction of nuclear and mixed-fuel power stations (oil and gas). The highest level of consensus was reached regarding development and use of public transport in towns, especially in Europe.

This historic phase was to last 10–15 years and it brought with it profound changes in the world of energy. During this same period, however, certain events took place, which at the time had little relevance but nevertheless triggered important transformations in the following decades.

In 1974 the International Energy Agency (IEA) was created; an association between the main oil consuming countries with two fundamental purposes:

- To mutually assist one another in the case of an embargo (for political reasons) by the cartel of crude producing countries. No one wished to see the affair of 1973 repeated.
- To exchange all possible information regarding national oil data (demand, supply, stocks, transport etc.), excluding those of a commercial nature (prices, trading activity etc.).

Having overcome the crisis of 1973, the IEA took the general role of a research bureau for energy issues unprecedented levels with its headquarters in Paris, countering the similar research bureau of OPEC headquartered in Vienna. It took some years before the work carried out proved to be of some use. The collection process for pertinent data from different countries took time and it was difficult to organize the information on efficient databases capable of updating in reasonable times.

Some years later, a new oilfield in the North Sea, named Brent, started production on 11 November 1976. On the following 13 December the first oil tanker left the terminal with a cargo of this crude, which would soon upset the balance of the world oil market.

And so we arrive at the events of 1979 characterized by the seizure of power by Saddam Hussein in Iraq, the revolution in Iran and the break-out of the Iran–Iraq war in September 1980. These events, and their subsequent consequences, mark the history of the oil market in the two following decades.

The start of the revolution in Iran was immediately seen as a serious threat to the geopolitical stability of the Persian Gulf area and a worrisome element of risk for the flow of crude exports towards the consumer countries.

Almost on tiptoes, all the oil companies in the world began to raise the level of their stocks in their storage and refineries, thus creating increased demand for crude precisely at the moment when production difficulties were felt in Iran. In this way a vicious circle was created which artificially raised the demand (to boost the stocks) and triggered a rise in prices. When the Iran–Iraq war broke out, in September 1980, it unleashed a true race for oil. All the bodies involved, among them oil companies, governments of consumer countries, industries and condominiums, pushed the level of stocks to the highest possible amounts. At the end of this rush the level of oil stocks in the western consumer countries had risen from the normal level, that is, what was needed to cover around 30–50 days' consumption, to that for 180 days, in other words five or six times greater than was necessary. One had even gone beyond the physical storage capacity on land. In the main ports supertankers were anchored and used as floating storage while waiting for tankage to become available onshore. Crude prices spiralled upwards, reaching levels of $40 per barrel for the lightest qualities.

The producing nations pushed their output up to unprecedented levels. Saudi Arabia reached the level of 11 million barrels per day, a record unrepeated thereafter. During the months of crisis some new mechanisms to protect the consumer countries were put into effect. The IEA, although having no reason to intervene operationally, by activating the assistance mechanism for countries in difficulty (there was no embargo or physical limitation on the supplies towards any of the member countries, but only a generalized rise in prices), began to make an essential contribution to governments and oil companies. The collection and examination of the statistical data showed clearly that the dramatic rise in prices was due to the simultaneous action in the same direction, without any coordination, of all those involved, causing a dramatic increase in the level of stocks of crude. Faced with the data that showed that the production system could function for 180 days using its stocks, even in the case of a total interruption of crude supplies, it was clear to everyone that the enormous costs incurred to maintain the stocks (logistic costs, finance charges) were completely unjustified and disproportionate. Further, the Iran–Iraq war had stalled and become by then a regional war, which could in no way affect the flow of oil supplies.

THE 1980s: THE GRADUAL DISAPPEARANCE OF OPEC

During 1982, all the oil companies in the world had drastically cut down their purchases of crude from the producing nations, particularly the OPEC ones, which continued to propose very aggressive prices. A new phase of the market opened up from this point. That phase, begun in

1973 with the rise of OPEC to leadership of the world oil market, came to an end and a new one of creeping crisis began: this, throughout the 1980s, led up to the loss of any role for OPEC and its member countries.

Faced with the facts that proved the dramatic excess of stocks, the OPEC countries were unable to find a common strategy to adjust production to the demand. At first they tried to force their customers to honour the current contracts, obliging them to take the same quantity of crude as in previous years, and then they began to use every kind of cunning to try to maintain the maximum levels of production of 1981. All the crude not purchased by the oil companies at the official prices (OSP) set by the OPEC conference was sold spot to independent traders at discounted market prices.

After several months of such practice, two parallel markets were actually created, one based on official prices and the other on spot prices. Thus, for the same type of crude there could be two prices, differing by as much as $10 per barrel. To remedy this situation, an extraordinary meeting was convened by OPEC, which resolved to reduce the official price of Arabian Light from $34 to $29 per barrel and to re-establish lower production quotas for its members. This decision was reached after furious discussions betweens the hawks (Iran at their head, who wanted to keep the price high) and the doves (headed by Saudi Arabia, who wanted to align with the real market).

The three following years were marked by a continuous weakening of crude prices, due to a combination of factors. After the crisis of 1973 the first effects of energy diversification began to become apparent with:

- The start-up of the new nuclear power stations, which began to cause a visible and progressive reduction in the consumption of fuel oil burned in the thermo-electric power stations, triggering a structural crisis in the refining system, particularly in Europe.
- An increase in the supplies of natural gas for electricity production as well as for domestic heating.

Refining capacity underwent a process of radical re-conversion and restructuring. The refineries found themselves at a crossroads: should they build cracking plants to transform fuel oil into gasoline and diesel fuel (thus improving refining margins), or shut down.

The production of the non-OPEC nations, historically marginal, began to become relevant and competitive on the international market. In particular, production in the North Sea began to play a key role in the political and economic balance in the oil world. These were the years when the prime minister of the United Kingdom was Margaret Thatcher, who wanted to deal a powerful blow on the excessive power of the OPEC countries. Thatcher's government refused any form of dialogue or cooperation with the OPEC countries tending to regulate crude prices by adjusting production. Together with the government of the USA, whose President was then Ronald Reagan, Mrs Thatcher wanted to reach the objective of having a crude oil price that was the result of free market transactions and without any political control by the OPEC cartel.

Finally it was the OPEC countries that, after the euphoria of the rise in prices during the previous decade, were not aware of the changes in the global energy and political scenario and continued to pump more oil into the market than the demand required, obviously violating the agreements within OPEC and fuelling the spot markets, parallel to the official ones.

THE PRICE WAR

The sole defence of the dignity of OPEC and the price level of the benchmark (Arabian Light) remained in the hands of Saudi Arabia, which in these years was forced to cut production from a rate of 11 million barrels per day in 1981 to scarcely 2.5 million in July 1985. A level so low as not to allow production of the gas associated, which, in turn, fed the structures of the producing plants. This sort of Babel continued until the summer of 1985.

One morning in late August 1985, Sheikh Yamani, the historic minister of Saudi Arabia, issued a declaration in which he claimed a fair market quota for his country, namely a production rate in line with the official OPEC agreement of about 5–6 million barrels per day. Yamani declared publicly and officially that the various OPEC countries were producing about 3 million barrels per day more to the detriment of Saudi Arabia and urged a return to a cartel regime. To make his message politically less explosive, two weeks later during a conference in Oxford regarding the oil market, he tried to draw attention towards the activities of the non-OPEC countries, particularly in the North Sea. These countries had hitherto refused any form of coordination of production levels, although in the meantime they had benefited from the high prices resulting from the Saudi sacrifices.

Yamani then announced a crude oil price war against the non-OPEC countries, even if it was clear that the main target was the OPEC countries that continued to flout the production quotas. To fight this war, Yamani informed the oil world that Saudi Arabia would, from that moment, adopt the following measures:

- Cessation of its role as swing producer to protect the benchmark price, that of Arabian Light.
- Renunciation by Saudi Arabia of the official price system (OSP) and refusal to publish or agree the price of Arabian Light.
- Adoption of a new price system for all Saudi crudes, based on their netback value.

This was a real upset in modern oil history, which illustrated all the hypocrisies that had allowed hitherto the maintenance of the unstable balance of the market.

Box 3.1   The Netback Value System

Let's make matters clear. What was the new netback value system adopted by Yamani?

It was a very simple way of increasing market share by destabilizing the price system and based on a very simple principle. A Saudi customer who signed the contract did not know the purchase price at the time he took away a cargo of crude. The price was established at the end of the customer's production and marketing cycle, after he had sold in the market the finished products obtained from refining the Saudi crude. The price to pay the Saudis was established with a calculation of this type:

a. Revenue obtained from sale of finished products	100
b. Costs incurred for transport of crude	5
c. Costs incurred for refining crude	5
d. Finance and other charges	4
e. Guaranteed margin for customer	10
Price to pay for crude $(P = a - b - c - d - e)$	76

A mechanism was set up by which every purchaser of Saudi crude who had an integrated downstream system (refining and sale of finished products) earned a guaranteed fixed margin on every barrel of crude purchased, apart from the profits derived from the optimum management of his operations. Thus, the more barrels he managed to obtain from the producing country, the greater were his profits.

No great analysis is needed to understand that, when this mechanism was announced, sales of Saudi crudes increased and a queue of customers lined up to sign the new contracts.

What about the other producing countries? The OPEC countries waited just to understand the new mechanism before competing with the Saudis. Hence, they began to sell their crude with the same pricing mechanism, perhaps increasing the guaranteed margin for the purchaser.

A situation of total liberty from the production restrictions of OPEC and the defence of the price level occurred. The euphoria of the petrodollars obscured any powers of analysis and comprehension of the collective interests of the producing countries. Monopoly conditions no longer existed in the oil market. The free market had begun to operate in a context of full competition between OPEC and non-OPEC producers. The market dynamics changed from the so-called oligopoly model, which obeyed the classical law that links price to supply and quickly, and a competitive free market was created.

1985–2000: FROM THE INTRODUCTION OF BRENT AS AN INTERNATIONAL BENCHMARK TO THE CLEAN AIR ACT

The inevitable arrived unexpectedly quickly. Actually, the process triggered had very precise and inexorable features. Yamani, in his unleashed war of prices, had brought to his side all the producing countries and all the refiners in the world, who, unknowingly and in a climate of collective folly, continued to pump crude and finished products into the market as fast as possible.

The crisis of the mechanism began when the market, flooded with finished products, was no longer able to absorb further quantities. The price of these products therefore began to fall and dragged the price of crude down with it, mathematically linked to that of the products, engendering a climate of confusion and frenetic activity by the oil professionals.

Right at that time and in that mood of conflict, an alternative solution for fixing the price of crude in a free market context came from the North Sea. In July 1986, one year after Yamani's declaration, Shell UK published the '15 day Brent contract' (later we shall give a detailed description of this new market mechanism). For the first time the price of crude, Brent, was anchored to a sort of petroleum exchange, where a selected number of professionals (about 100) could operate, helping to define, day by day, the price level. It was not yet a world reference point, only regional and very limited to the north European sphere. However, in a very short time it became the reference tool in the London marketplace, where all the oil trading companies, linked to the big oil companies or independent operators, had their headquarters and carried out their business activities.

In this complex scenario, each single world event, any form of tension in the Middle East and any decision by the OPEC countries in the London atmosphere kindled the expectations of the market and pushed Brent upwards or downwards, influencing positively or negatively the crude price levels of the OPEC countries. Specifically, the movements of the Brent market became very critical for the price levels of Nigerian crudes, that is, those of the highest quality among the crudes of the OPEC nations and very similar to Brent. The Nigerian crudes were caught between two fires:

- on one side the need to keep the price differential vis-à-vis Arabian Light at least $4–5 per barrel higher; and
- on the other, to compete with Brent which was priced at least $1–2 per barrel lower.

For a country like Nigeria, already saddled with a serious financial crisis and exposed to massive immigration from the neighbouring countries, the direct competition with the North Sea was disastrous. Especially because the two types of crude were competing for the same profitable US market.

Putting the 15 day Brent contract on the market could not have come at a worse moment. In fact, it took place when the effects of the price war unleashed by Yamani were at their most devastating pitch. The tidal wave of over-full storage tanks was rising from consumer level (condominiums, industries) to distributor level and finally the refiners; everyone was convinced to fill up at ultra-convenient prices. When these levels began to jeopardize the operations and logistics of the refineries, the crash became inevitable.

At a speed hitherto unknown, prices began to tumble week after week and then day after day from the level of $30 per barrel down to $11 per barrel. This was the oil counter-shock. It was too much for everyone and especially for the heroic supporters of the free market for crude.

As long as there was OPEC to hold the crude price level at around $28–30 per barrel, to speak of a free market only meant a free fluctuation of the daily oscillations of a few dollars per barrel on stock markets. But now the picture was different and dramatic. In London they spoke of a 'blood bath'. Many traders who had bought cargoes of crude only a few days earlier at prices considered good at the time were forced to sell these cargoes at $10 or $20 per barrel under the purchase price, with massive losses in consequence. The big companies honoured commitments in any case, but many independent traders preferred to declare bankruptcy and disappeared from the market.

The producing countries witnessed for the first time after more than a decade the crash of oil revenues and were forced to make drastic cuts in their investment and expense budgets. The effect of these cuts made itself felt in the economies of the industrialized countries, who found themselves missing, from one day to another, contracts and tenders that were finalized. The oil companies were forced to block their development investments in areas where the production costs would have been higher than the new level of crude prices. Production in a series of marginal fields had to stop since they were no longer profitable.

In the USA about 2 million barrels per day of crude production coming from the so-called *strippers*, those tiny fields in the back garden that we see in films of that period, disappeared from the national oil balance sheet.

The North Sea suffered a severe cutback in the development of the existing fields and a freeze-up of research projects.

In Nigeria the crisis was such as to cause an exodus of biblical dimensions: over 20 million persons returned to the neighbouring countries they had come from 20 years earlier.

One thing was clear to everyone: the price of crude, left free to move only on the basis of the laws of the free market, had fallen to a level that allowed the supply to vary in line with the demand, in other words, to a level so low as to eliminate all the marginal fields, whose production cost was higher than the going price. This price level, however, was not compatible with the equilibrium of the world economy and politics, and it was also not compatible with the guarantees for future supplies. The free market was not compatible with the oil market. A solution had to be found – quickly.

During 1987 meetings were held at various levels between the players involved, OPEC and non-OPEC countries, governments of consumer countries and producing countries. Everything pointed in one direction only, a return to a protected system for crude prices, with OPEC guaranteeing stability.

In December 1987, Saudi Arabia agreed to sign the new agreement between the OPEC countries that envisaged the return to the system of official prices with Arabian Light in the role of benchmark, which was fixed at \$28 per barrel. In the space of around three months the market stabilized and the crude price returned to the levels programmed by the OPEC countries. Encouraged by this political result and the new cohesion shown by its member countries, OPEC required that even the non-OPEC countries should indicate their willingness to make some contribution towards modulating supply. However, during the meetings that followed in 1987 and 1988, no significant results were achieved.

On the contrary, a further step was taken in the process of transforming the physical market for Brent into a purely financial market. The price crash in 1986 had created a climate of panic in the London petroleum and financial circles. The 15 day contract had proved not to be fully adequate to guarantee the economic and financial system and had caused the bankruptcy of dozens of trading companies declared insolvent. The biggest companies producing Brent Blend (Shell, Exxon, Chevron and BP) had had to re-purchase the cargoes of Brent not collected and abandoned by the traders who were wiped out. The costs of the crisis turned out to be enormous for the economic and financial system of the City. The intention had been to create a purely financial Brent market, in which there was no longer any obligation for the participants to buy a physical cargo of crude, but only to handle financial paper.

In July 1988, the IPE (International Petroleum Exchange) launched the Brent Futures contract. The event was hailed as the long-sought solution finally found, the new frontier of the free oil market vis-à-vis the archaic solutions proposed by OPEC (the return to the system of official prices).

THE SUICIDE OF OPEC

The lack of agreement on production control and the propaganda at the point of provocation regarding the unsophisticated economic vision of the OPEC countries caused a new serious and irreversible crisis in the government of the international oil market.

In December 1988 OPEC, guided by Saudi Arabia, decided to accept the challenge of modernity and the free oil market that everyone desired, abandoning yet again the OSP system and adopting as the new benchmark Brent itself.

All the crudes produced by the OPEC nations were from that time to be priced with reference to Brent. The various countries would limit themselves to setting the price differential to apply to each crude vis-à-vis the market value of Brent. For a pure question of national pride, what was commonly called the price differential vis-à-vis the benchmark was re-named OSP by the OPEC countries, although it was quite clear that the crude price was no longer published, but only its adjustment vis-à-vis the benchmark, in other words a more or less negligible fraction of the price of a particular crude.

The event was hailed positively by all the commentators and the market operators. It seemed the end of a sort of Middle Ages and a step towards a much-desired new world. However, all the upsets and immediate consequences that the change would bring were not appreciated. Neither was it understood, in the euphoria and the desire to proclaim a political victory, that in fact the OPEC countries had tried to start a new price war using the Brent market as a tool (leaving aside the net-back used in 1986).

The OPEC, in turn, did not understand that, having started this war in the political climate of those times, it did not have great hopes of victory and in fact its decision turned out to be a real act of suicide. From that time, OPEC lost any reason to exist. It was transformed into a cooperative study bureau between the member countries, prestigious but with no other operational role: a sort of rival project to the IEA.

The truth was that since all the producing nations in the OPEC and non-OPEC world used the same benchmark, actually they were all part of the same non-existent cartel. But since this ghostly cartel had no agreement for regulating supply, there was no way to discipline or control the prices. The market had become absolutely free, just as Mrs Thatcher and the City of London had so much desired.

THE START OF THE FREE MARKET

The sequence of market events quickly showed the inconsistency of the analyses that had convinced the majority to celebrate the OPEC decision. In the absence of any agreement between the producers, everyone felt free to produce as much as they could and to try to sell their crude in competition with the others, simply varying the price differential vis-à-vis Brent (thus, the concept of variable discount was born). What happened seemed an exact replica of 1986 events. The price of the new benchmark, Brent, dropped quickly to around $9 per barrel.

It is interesting to read again the remarks of the most important commentators of the time; after preaching modernity and acceptance of the principles of the free market by OPEC, after the price crashed down to \$9 per barrel, they began to criticize the lack of cohesion between the OPEC countries and their incapacity to control production levels. It became clear that an oil market only apparently free was desired, but actually supported by voluntary production cuts by OPEC (which had committed suicide in December 1988).

The acceleration of the crisis was also aggravated by the end of the Iran–Iraq war, which took place at this time. The two ex-belligerents, both in a profound financial crisis, had dire need to increase their production and crude oil revenues to reconstruct their countries. They asked the other Gulf countries to give back their market outlets which had been taken up during the war by Kuwait, the Emirates, Saudi Arabia and Venezuela in particular. The reply from the countries concerned was totally negative (we should not forget the new general context of the market when this happened), with the result that the newly increased production from Iran and Iraq contributed to flood the markets.

It was absolutely necessary to reduce world crude production and therefore to find a swing producer. All attempts to find one, who would come forward willingly, either as an individual country (as Saudi Arabia had done between 1982 and 1985) or as a collective entity (OPEC), had failed. OPEC in fact no longer existed after December 1988, when it had adopted Brent as benchmark. Political history and the military events in the Persian Gulf area took charge from that time and for over a decade chose the swing producer of the international oil market.

This historic phase began in August 1989 with the invasion of Kuwait by Iraq. Rivers of ink have been used to describe this event and its aftermath lasting over two decades. This war is still loaded with political consequences and is far from receiving a historic judgement that is not interpreted as politically biased. As it affects our tale, let's show how the price model worked in that context.

Formally we were, in fact, in a free market system, with the distinction that reduction of supply was the task of a swing producer imposed by a real situation and not by the decision of a political–economic cartel. Above all, it was clear that the nomination of a swing producer was not made with the agreement of the nominee. The result, from the technical and economic standpoint, was, however, to lessen the pressure of supply on the market, allowing prices to be stabilized in the region of \$15–20 per barrel. The first candidate for the role of swing producer was Kuwait, who, for almost two or three years was no longer able to produce, thus removing from the market over 2 million barrels per day.

We should repeat that from the economic point of view the market had remained a free market, with an outside limit (stoppage of production from Kuwait) not programmed by any cartel, and not imposed (even if not unwelcome) by market forces.

The first Gulf War triggered the next baton change. Kuwait passed the relay baton to Iraq, which became the swing producer, obliged and official, of the oil world for almost a decade. During the change of baton, before the outbreak of the Gulf War, the price reached $40 per barrel. It was a short-lived peak, more an exchange speculation of the emotional sort that had no real effect on crude movements, almost a celebration of the event itself. The same night that the bombardment of Baghdad began, the price tumbled from $40 to the usual $16–20 per barrel.

The UN embargo on Iraq had the result that the re-start of production in Kuwait was compensated by the stoppage of exports from Iraq, with a substantial balancing of the volumes. This equilibrium lasted till 1996, when growth of demand and the aftermath of the Chernobyl accident began to nudge the crude price over the $20 per barrel range, finally touching and exceeding $25 per barrel.

It was right at this moment that the debate over the humanitarian aspect in Iraq heated up and began to gather a global consensus in the media. In this new climate, the Security Council of the United Nations (UN) approved a resolution that permitted Iraq to sell limited quantities of crude to purchase food and essential goods, the so-called oil for food programme. The resolution envisaged a duration of six months, with eventual renewals to decide duration and amount of crude to export.

Without going into the political merit of the matter, we have to note that – always from the technical and economic standpoints – the flow of Iraq crude into the market had the effect of maintaining price stability in the desired range of $16–20 per barrel.

In 1998 there was disagreement between Iraq and the UN inspectors, who left the country. Iraq declared it was no longer open for dialogue with the UN unless the cycle of inspections and the sanctions were terminated. At the same time it began to boost to the maximum possible (for the state of the plants and the pipeline network) the production and export of crude, favouring certain marketing channels outside the official control of the UN. The arrival of these extra barrels came at a critical time for the market, right at the time when the increased production from non-OPEC countries (North Sea, Angola and Kazakhstan) and other OPEC countries (Nigeria, Venezuela, Algeria etc.) was being felt.

Once again the conditions were created for a fall in the crude price, this time faster than in the past, bearing in mind that the financial markets had assumed the role of accelerator to this course of action.

In 1999 the price of Brent stood at $9 per barrel, the lowest in the last 20 years. This level, however, was no longer considered by all the analysts, oil companies and producing countries, as a temporary event or the fruit of a crisis easy to overcome, but rather as a structural reality, due, in a free market situation, to the constant excess of supply over demand.

All the budgets of producer nations and oil companies are drawn up in the shadow of cuts in costs and investments. In this scenario, many oil companies adopted dramatic rationalization programmes that also involved mergers with their competitors. The most overt cases were Exxon-Mobil, Total-Fina-Elf, BP-Amoco-Arco and Chevron-Texaco.

Actually, all these analyses and forecasts, even if they have been glaringly contradicted by history (only a few months afterwards), were apparently correct. We were in conditions of an excess of crude supply over demand for at least two decades and in the absence of any cartel whatsoever, which might have regulated the offer. The price, therefore, could only stay low.

THE CONSEQUENCES OF THE ENVIRONMENTAL TURNAROUND

Nobody foresaw the small (yet big) revolution that the implementation of the Clean Air Act in the USA, enacted during 1999 to take effect from 1 January 2000, would have sparked off in all the world oil markets. This measure tore from the hand of the mystical and mysterious architect the pencil that from the 1960s until then had enabled him to trace the graph of the price of crude.

4

Changes in the Market for Automotive Fuels

EVOLUTION OF ENVIRONMENTAL DEMAND

The most notable effect of the Chernobyl accident on 26 April 1986 was the halt in construction programmes for nuclear power stations across the entire world. There were, however, other effects deriving from the emotions aroused by that dramatic event, which were not discussed at any length but which caused, in the course of time, enormous modifications in the world energy configuration.

The debate over environmental problems had actually been ventilated some time ago in certain countries. We might remember the success of Rachel Carson's 1962 book *Silent Spring*, which revealed the global effects of the inconsiderate use of DDT (*dichlorodiphenyltrichloroethane*) and the first Earth Day organized in the USA on 22 April 1970.

The primary emotional effect, subsequently removed, was the silence which fell on the word energy. This word became a sort of taboo in every political speech and in the programmes of the various governments of the industrialized nations, and it was completely replaced by the word environment. The total separation between the two problems has produced results that we are paying dearly for today. Actually, a sort of conception has grown up in which the objective of improving the environment seems to be just a cultural choice desired or rejected for ideological reasons, independently of technology and economics.

The day after Chernobyl set in motion, among other actions, a legislative process which imposed on all the industrialized nations, apart from the nuclear moratorium, a change in fuel specifications, in particular for automotive fuels.

No measure, however, bothered to check how, if and at what costs the industry would be able to make an adequate response to the new quality requirements of the market. No-one raised the problem of how to encourage the investments needed and how to make the industry an informed and motivated protagonist of the environmental changes suggested.

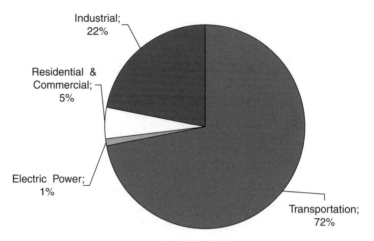

Figure 4.1 USA crude demand by sector (2009)

Source: U.S. Energy Information Administration

Figure 4.1 shows crude demand in the USA by sector.

The aftermath of Chernobyl highlighted certain trends in the oil sector (see Tables 4.1 and 4.2 and Figure 4.2), in particular:

- A massive increase in world oil consumption.
- A tightening of environmental specifications for all fuels, with dire effects on those for the automotive sector.
- A growing inadequacy of the world refining system vis-à-vis the changes that had taken place.

We shall examine each of these aspects in depth, to grasp how they are behind the current international energy crisis.

Some 25 years after Chernobyl, the world oil balance has undergone the transformations shown in Table 4.3.

Table 4.1 Evolution of gasoline specifications

	Aromatics		Olephines		Benzene		Sulphur	
	Europe %	USA %	Europe %	USA %	Europe %	USA %	Europe ppm	USA ppm
1995					5		1000/500	320
2000	42	45	18	18	1	4	150	150
2005	35	35	18		1	1	50(10)	30
2010	35	25	18	6	1	1	10	10

Table 4.2   Evolution of gasoil specifications

	Poliaromatics		Sulphur		Density	
	Europe %	USA %	Europe ppm	USA ppm	Europe kg/m³	USA kg/m³
1995			2000/500	5000	820–860	
2000	11	11	350	500	820–845	
2005	11	11	50/10	15/50	820–845	
2010	8(6)		10	15	820–845	

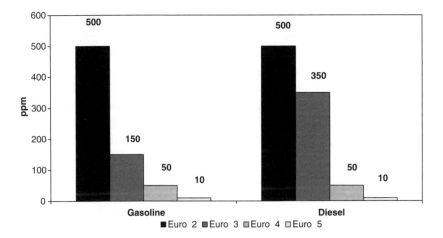

Figure 4.2   Evolution of gasoil specifications

Table 4.3   World crude oil demand

	1986	2010	2010−1986
World Oil Demand (million bbl/day)	60.0	87.7	**27.7**
Of which:			
North America	15.7	23.9	8.2
Europe	12.6	14.4	1.8
Asia Pacific	10.4	27.4	17.0

Source: International Energy Agency

Oil demand has grown by 27.7 million barrels per day, of which 17 million serve to cover the growth of the Asiatic countries, under 2 million for the European nations and 8.2 million for the USA. Table 4.3 shows this distribution in the course of almost 25 years. It can be seen that while Europe has to some extent stabilized its oil demand, the USA and the Asian countries continue their process of growth and capture of the oil reserves available. Moreover the USA must face up to another structural emergency, namely the continual fall in domestic production of crude, which has gone from 8.9 to 5.1 million barrels per day, for a net reduction of 3.8 million barrels per day. It is as if the USA had cut down its productive capacity by an amount equal to the production of Iran, the second OPEC producing nation. These data appear to show the extent of the leadership crisis which has dogged America in the past decade.

There is a mixture of lack of awareness of the data of the problem and a sort of subjection to the petroleum lobby, which has taken some kind of revenge against the European countries, free to expand their activities in areas of the world forbidden to the US companies (e.g. Iran, Iraq, Libya). In this context few have understood the need to exploit the new frontiers of technology for both production and consumption of energy. And so, with these changes, the internal structure of consumption in the various areas of the world has marked up an incomprehensible growth in per capita consumption in the USA from 24 to almost 26 barrels per year in 2007 then brought down to 23 merely due to the contingent economic crises, while in Europe it has remained steady at the 1985 level at 9.6 barrels per year. The Asian countries are light-years away, although they have gone from 1.12 to 1.72 barrels per year. Perhaps one day, in 10 years perhaps, China and India will become a problem for their competition on the energy and oil market, but today the situation is very different (and there is plenty of time to get suitably organized).

Analysis of the data in Figures 4.3 and 4.4 is fundamental to understand the internal dynamics of the oil market and the impact of the changes in environmental legislation enacted after Chernobyl.

The first actions regarding fossil fuels were taken in almost all the industrialized nations (including Japan), with the banning of leaded gasolines (an additive for raising the octane number, but very poisonous and pollutant) and proceeding to the reduction of the sulphur content. The real jump forward in quality came in 1990 with the approval in the USA of the Clean Air Act, which introduced a revolution in the composition of gasolines, with the so-called reformulated types.

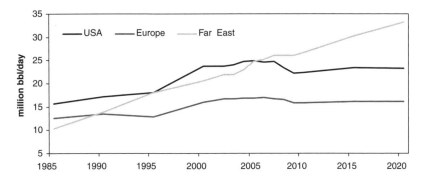

Figure 4.3 Evolution of oil demand in the USA, Europe and Asia-Pacific (1985–2020)
Source: International Energy Agency

Actually, two types of decisions were taken regarding the quality of automotive fuels:

- To continue with the limitation and elimination of contaminant substances (total banning of lead, continual reduction of sulphur content and oxygenated compounds).
- To intervene regarding the molecular composition of the hydrocarbons used in fuels, setting the maximum content of those types of hydrocarbons considered to be health risks.

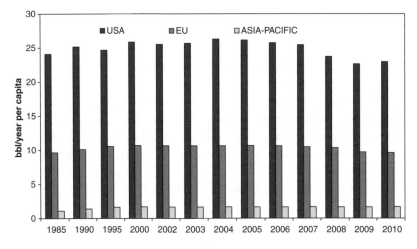

Figure 4.4 Per capita oil demand in the USA, Europe and Asia-Pacific (1985–2010)
Sources: International Energy Agency, United Nations

The revolution inherent in these decisions was not immediately grasped by the industry and the authorities themselves that had proposed them. In fact, the date for implementation of the law was fixed as from January 1996, giving six years of grace to the operators to organize themselves. However, the lack of perception of the future impact on the oil industry gave no clue that powerful incentives would be required to motivate the companies to invest in the transformation of their plants. Without incentives and without the start of any industrial re-conversion process, it became clear that after the six years leading up to 1996, the American refining industry was not able to respond to the new specifications imposed by the Clean Air Act; it was therefore necessary to postpone the implementation for a further four years, namely to January 2000.

In 1999, in the middle of the American presidential election campaign (Gore versus Bush), the problem was re-proposed in exactly the same terms as in 1996: that is, American industry was not ready to respond to the market changes which would derive from application of the new law. This time, however, the political conditions were not such as to allow a further postponement. The Greens exerted pressure and furthermore one independent Green politician from Florida was a candidate for the Presidency and seemed capable of filching some important votes from Gore, the democratic candidate who was challenging Bush. A deferment of the Clean Air Act, passed by the Clinton administration, would have been fatal for Gore. Thus, the American administration confirmed the implementation of the new law from the starting date envisaged of 1 January 2000.

The impact on the US and world oil markets was dramatic. A rise in prices began, which didn't stop until the financial crisis of autumn 2008. Actually, a situation arose in which crude prices broke away from the control of any organ whatever (OPEC, oil companies, nations).

But what made application of the new law impracticable or difficult? And why was its introduction so momentous for the evolution of crude oil prices?

To make an adequate reply we have to consider some technical aspects of the problem in depth.

GASOLINE AND ITS COMPONENTS

What is commonly called gasoline is a mixture of several components, obtained through the refining process of crude oil. These components,

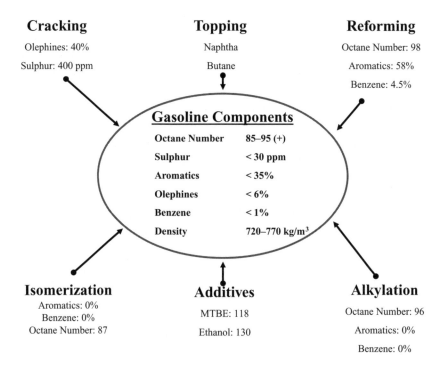

Cracking

Olephines: 40%

Sulphur: 400 ppm

Topping

Naphtha

Butane

Reforming

Octane Number: 98

Aromatics: 58%

Benzene: 4.5%

Gasoline Components

Octane Number	**85–95 (+)**
Sulphur	**< 30 ppm**
Aromatics	**< 35%**
Olephines	**< 6%**
Benzene	**< 1%**
Density	**720–770 kg/m³**

Isomerization

Aromatics: 0%
Benzene: 0%
Octane Number: 87

Additives

MTBE: 118

Ethanol: 130

Alkylation

Octane Number: 96

Aromatics: 0%

Benzene: 0%

Figure 4.5   Gasoline and refining plants

and their quality, vary as a function of the complexity of the technological cycle and the size of the refinery producing them, as well as the
crude oils (the raw material) available for processing.

This problem will be examined later in more detail. At this stage,
however, we shall confine ourselves to listing the refinery plants dedicated to gasoline production and the characteristics of the components
obtained from each plant (see Figure 4.5).

In the annexed sketch we give an example of a refinery, quite complex,
but more or less in line with the medium–high standards of the oil
industry at present. We see clearly that the components for blending
gasolines come from five separate plants, each one producing a different
component with different characteristics.

Reforming

Reforming is the key plant for producing gasoline and it is present in all
refineries, even the most simple and traditional ones. Its function is to

transform the molecules of linear hydrocarbons into molecules of more complex, cyclical form to increase the octane number, which at the end of the treatment exceeds the limit of 85–95 required for commercial gasoline. The component produced is called reformed gasoline. The chemical–physical reactions which permit the increase in octane number have the undesired effect of increasing the amounts of benzenes and aromatics well beyond the acceptable limits of the new norms. Thus, gasoline obtained in a refinery having only this plant could not be marketed, because although satisfactory as regards octane number it would contain too much benzene and aromatics.

This is an example where the new norms have made it almost impossible for a traditional refinery to produce gasoline on specification. To formulate an acceptable gasoline these refineries would have to buy component products elsewhere, to be able to mix them with the reformed gasoline; alternatively they could focus their purchases of crude on those types which allow creation of semi-finished products which permit formulation of acceptable gasoline. This option, however, is not easy, since it is obvious that all refineries with such problems are continually trying to get their hands on these crudes, whose availability is limited and whose prices are very high.

Cracking

Cracking is the plant which enables a significant increase in the volume of gasoline produced, through a process which converts heavy fractions of petroleum into light products (gasoline, gasoil). Development of such plants was accelerated in the 1980s, when the demand for fuel oil from the power stations was greatly reduced, following the construction of nuclear power stations and the transformation of oil-burning power stations into stations burning natural gas (methane). With the refining systems then in use, about 50% of heavy fuel oil was obtained from crude oil. When demand for this fell, it became essential to equip refineries with plants to transform it into other light products, demand for which was, on the contrary, rising fast. Thus, a series of cracking plants (with various technologies) were devised, all aimed at increasing the production of gasoline and gasoil by transforming heavy fuel oil. Needless to say, these plants are those which guarantee the highest profitability within a refinery. In fact the price ratio between the products obtained (gasoline and gasoil) and the feedstocks used (heavy fuel oil) is on average three to one, but it can also reach higher levels.

Yet, even in this case, there is a problem of quality. These gasolines have high olephines content (unstable products, therefore dangerous, obtained by splitting heavy molecules). The new norms limit this content quite drastically to a maximum of 6%. This puts a strict limit on the refining process cycle as it has been structured in the last decades.

Alkylation

Obviously, there is a technological answer to this problem. This is the construction of an alkylation plant downstream of the cracking unit. Actually, this plant produces, starting from the waste olefinic gases from the cracking unit, a gasoline of very high quality, with a high octane number, without benzenes, without sulphur, without aromatics. This is a costly and dangerous plant. It operates at a pressure of over 40 atmospheres and it is full of sulphuric acid. Any accident could be fatal. To obtain a permit to insert it in existing refineries, perhaps close to inhabited centres, is certainly not easy. During the gasoline season (April–August), the price of alkylate gasoline reaches unbelievable levels ($100–200 per tonne) above those for reformed gasoline.

Isomerization

Another minor production process is isomerization, which contributes towards the slight increase in the octane number of the light virgin naphtha produced by the topping unit. This is, however, a marginal contribution both in quantity and in quality. The octane number of the isomerate gasoline is in fact close to the minimum required for marketing. The plant enables the light virgin naphtha to be used up, particularly if the amount produced is limited and cannot be commercialized for other uses (in petrochemicals). On the other hand it does not raise the octane number enough to 'absorb' other products of lower quality in the mixture of gasolines.

REFINERS WALK THE TIGHTROPE

On the basis of what we have seen so far, we can understand that the quantity of components for gasoline produced every day in a refinery can (with difficulty) be mixed together and automatically create a gasoline ready for sale on the final market (US or European). In fact, the overall resulting quality is compatible with the technical characteristics required by the engines (octane number, density) and by environmental norms (sulphur, aromatics, benzenes and olephines).

Many of the problems in balancing quality were and still are solved by adding to the mixture certain so-called oxygenated compounds, namely MTBE (*Methyl tert-butyl ether*) or other similar products. In the USA, inclusion of MTBE in gasoline has been prohibited since 2006, making the life of refiners harder still.

Let us now imagine that a US refinery, with this technology available and with the environmental norms operative, must be able to supply its hinterland with a variety of about 40 different types of gasoline, each one formulated to specifications among the strangest and restrictive possible. The task becomes a nightmare, which can be faced only through a frenetic purchase activity for specific components imported from other international markets (e.g. Europe, South America). Obviously the price of these components becomes sky-high during the gasoline season and causes a reduced availability of high-quality product in the markets of those areas that produce but also export these components. This is why the price of gasoline in Europe is practically in line with that in the USA (net of taxes), instead of being much lower, the market having a big surplus of product (see Figure 4.6).

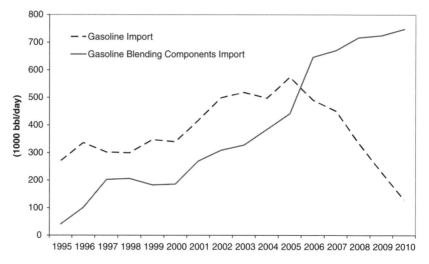

Figure 4.6   USA imports: gasoline versus blending components

Source: U.S. Energy Information Administration

This mechanism, previously described, might appear to be an irrelevant technical detail for the experts concerned. On the contrary, however, it represents the crux of the problem of understanding today's dynamics of the international oil market. The need to restock the biggest and richest world oil market with marginal products creates competition at global level, a sort of continuous but invisible auction, in which the product is assigned to the highest bidder, to the person or firm able to pay the highest price. But with the result that the price of the last barrel of product sold becomes the market price of that day for the whole world. The proof of this phenomenon is before our eyes:

- The gasoline price in the European countries, producers of surplus gasoline and exporters to the US markets, turns out to be in line with the very high price in the USA (net of taxes). All the investments made in the refining sector and the price paid in terms of industrial pollution do not generate any economic benefit for European consumers.
- The poorer countries of Africa and the Middle East (often important crude producing countries but without a significant refining activity) find themselves, during the US gasoline season, very short of product and with consequential social problems (e.g. Iran, Nigeria, Egypt, Angola).
- A dual gasoline market has thus developed a US market and a European market, comprising high-quality gasoline and low-quality gasoline made by blending low-specification components not saleable in industrialized countries.

This is a precarious balance which has been maintained with great difficulty and which has already shown the potential disasters that financial speculation can create (starting from this). Action in the refining sector has now become urgent and inevitable, but unfortunately, as we shall see later, it will not be taken for some time yet (Figure 4.7 shows a simplified refinery scheme). We shall, therefore, have to learn how to consider the oil price with a completely different mental model and leave the producing countries in peace when things do not work as we would like.

THE FISCAL POLICY OF THE INDUSTRIALIZED COUNTRIES REGARDING FUELS

It is important to note that, when faced with the structural problems that we have just mentioned, the governments of the industrialized

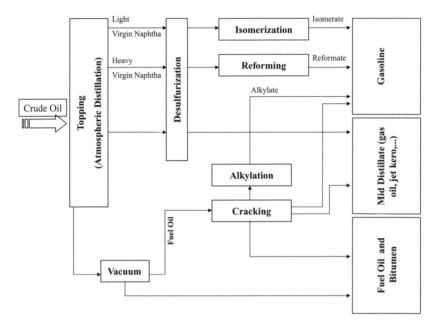

Figure 4.7 Simplified refinery scheme

countries, instead of focusing on the quest for a stable and integrated solution using policies of incentives for industrial investments and research projects, have in fact contributed towards amplifying the effect of the crisis through taxation on fuels so punitive as to justify our saying that effectively *the real automotive fuel is composed of taxes.*

This matter is deeply felt by consumers of oil, in particular the motorists of the various countries who suffer the effects and costs of the phenomena just examined. It is true that the reactions of the public are often emotional and based on the well-worn clichés, usually for ignorance of the real mechanisms that affect the prices of crude and finished products, and even more regarding the taxation of petroleum products imposed by the governments of the consumer countries. This in fact constitutes one of the fundamental variables for determining the true cost afflicting the consumers and the economies of the industrialized nations. The tax burden is often much greater than the sum of the costs of the raw material, its transformation and distribution as finished products.

The OPEC countries have always strongly criticized the governments of the industrialized nations for their fiscal policies, seen as amplifiers and accelerators of the processes that have made crude oil prices completely irrational. And the fact that the reactions of the consumer are often the result of unawareness of the real mechanisms is important. The taxation of petroleum products imposed by the governments of the consumer nations is one of the fundamental variables for determining the true cost afflicting the consumers and the economies of the industrialized nations. We may well say that the final consumers have no real perception of the cost of crude oil, since the major charge affecting them is the taxation on finished products, which, being a fixed percentage of their industrial cost, is greatly magnified with every increase in the crude oil price.

Regarding this issue even the producing nations accuse the governments of the industrialized countries of adopting a tax policy on oil so punitive as to make the effective price level of the raw material completely immaterial. The system of continually putting the blame on the producing nations is considered unacceptable, when the greater part of the price increases at the retail level is due in fact to taxation. Perhaps a better knowledge of the taxation mechanisms on gasoline and diesel, with a clear statement of the amounts and their effect on consumption, would avoid concentrating the blame on the producing countries and the oil companies, but without keeping the governments responsible for such tax policies out of the picture.

Perhaps it will be useful to give some consideration to the concrete data in Table 4.4 regarding the oil sector, comparing two different realities – the European and the American – which historically have used two different philosophies concerning the taxation of automotive fuels.

It is interesting to comment on some of the data which emerge.

The average list price applied by the oil companies in Europe is higher than that in the USA. This is in clear contrast with the fact that a significant proportion of US gasoline is imported from Europe. It is well known that European structure produces excess gasoline, while the US market has a deficit of over a million barrels per day. Based on the laws of economics it would be reasonable to expect that gasoline in the USA would cost more than that in Europe, at least to compensate for the transport cost from the Mediterranean/North Europe to the Atlantic coast of the USA. Surprisingly, the contrary happens. *It is just as if the price of lemons were higher in Sicily and Spain than in Norway and Sweden.*

The taxation on gasoline in Europe represents around 60% of the price at the pump and about 136% of the market price, while in the USA it is only 13% of the price at the pump and 15% of the market price.

Table 4.4 Gasoline in Europe and the USA: list price and price at the pump

	Retail premium gasoline prices				Retail premium gasoline taxes				Retail premium gasoline prices			
	UE		USA		UE		USA		UE		USA	
	(€/liter)	Δ %	(€/liter)	Δ %	(€/liter)	Δ %	(€/liter)	Δ %	(€/liter)	Δ %	(€/liter)	Δ %
2000	0.35		0.34		0.77		0.13		1.12		0.48	
2001	0.32	−9%	0.34	−1%	0.76	−1%	0.14	3%	1.08	−3%	0.48	0%
2002	0.30	−7%	0.30	−12%	0.77	1%	0.13	−5%	1.06	−1%	0.43	−10%
2003	0.30	1%	0.30	1%	0.77	0%	0.11	−17%	1.06	0%	0.41	−4%
2004	0.34	14%	0.33	12%	0.80	4%	0.10	−9%	1.14	7%	0.43	6%
2005	0.42	23%	0.42	27%	0.82	3%	0.10	2%	1.24	9%	0.52	21%
2006	0.48	13%	0.49	15%	0.83	1%	0.10	−3%	1.31	5%	0.59	12%
2007	0.49	4%	0.49	0%	0.85	2%	0.09	−8%	1.34	3%	0.58	−1%
2008	0.57	15%	0.55	12%	0.85	0%	0.09	−4%	1.42	6%	0.64	10%
2009	0.41	−27%	0.37	−32%	0.82	−4%	0.12	38%	1.24	−13%	0.49	−23%
2010	0.53	28%	0.51	37%	0.86	5%	0.09	−22%	1.39	13%	0.60	23%

Source: U.S. Energy Information Administration

Table 4.5 Price of gasoline and diesel fuel in some European countries

€/liter Jan 10–Sept 10	Prices (excluding taxes)		Taxes		Pump prices	
	Gasoline	Diesel	Gasoline	Diesel	Gasoline	Diesel
UK	0.36	0.44	0.87	0.87	1.36	1.38
Netherlands	0.56	0.56	0.96	0.62	1.52	1.18
Italy	0.55	0.57	0.79	0.61	1.34	1.18
France	0.52	0.55	0.84	0.62	1.36	1.17
Germany	0.54	0.56	0.89	0.66	1.42	1.22
Belgium	0.55	0.56	0.85	0.57	1.40	1.13
Luxembourg	0.54	0.54	0.62	0.44	1.15	0.98
Spain	0.55	0.56	0.59	0.50	1.14	1.06
Ireland	0.52	0.55	0.78	0.66	1.31	1.21
Average	**0.52**	**0.54**	**0.80**	**0.62**	**1.33**	**1.17**

Source: UK Petroleum Industry Association Ltd.

The consequence of these two different situations is that the retail price of gasoline in Europe is on average between two and three times higher than in the USA.

In Europe there is a heavier tax burden than in the USA, but with significant differences between one country and another (see Table 4.5).

In 2010, the list price applied by the companies (net of taxes) varied widely between each country: from €0.36 per litre in the UK to €0.56 per litre in the Netherlands.

In Italy the oil companies applied prices somewhat higher than the European average, €0.55 against €0.52 per litre, with the tax component in line with the European average and, thus, with the price at the pump slightly higher than the average in Europe.

It is not easy to obtain up-to-date and homogeneous data for all the countries in the world. However, the IEA has provided some important information regarding the main consuming countries for 2010.

The data shown in Figures 4.8 and 4.9, substantially in line with those from Europe in 2010, confirm some evident structural facts:

- The market price of gasoline is lower in the USA, Australia and the UK, countries which are net importers of finished products and where competition between the various operators is strong. We may note the situation in Australia, where, although there is no national oil company of importance, there is a very competitive system between the distributors, a high degree of transparency in the markets and a widespread institutional antitrust culture.

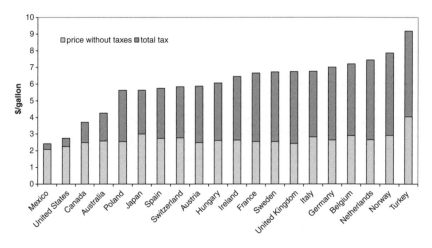

Figure 4.8   Gasoline prices in the world

Source: International Energy Agency

- In Italy, the most important refining country in the Mediterranean and a gasoline exporter, the consumer pays more for his or her gasoline than in all the other countries (apart from Norway, Turkey and Holland). Obviously the fragmentation of the distribution system and the high related costs play their part.

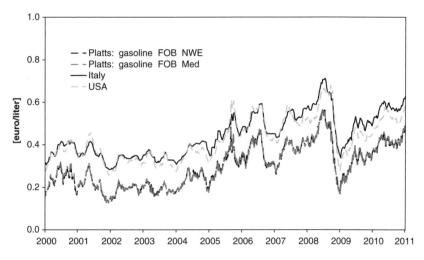

Figure 4.9   Price (excluding taxes) of gasoline in Europe and the USA

Sources: U.S. Energy Information Administration and European Commission

- The high taxation level in Europe means that the price of the industrial product (pre-tax) is low compared with the final price on the market, making less transparent and, thus, negligible the dynamics of the industry prices as well as competition between the operators. This phenomenon tends to worsen in countries where a culture rooted in transparency and effective antitrust control bodies is lacking.
- In the USA the gasoline price is closely aligned with the international market and responds quickly to the demand/supply balance. In 2008 we saw some cooling-off of the price (distance from the international market), while the price of the companies in Europe stayed at higher levels. The fall in the dollar/euro exchange rate should have caused the opposite effect, but actually it provided an additional benefit for the distributors and the Inland Revenue.

The same analysis can be made for gasoil with results quite similar to those of gasoline.

It is worthwhile examining the meaning of these differences in taxation policies for automotive fuels (see Figure 4.10). Transport policy in the USA has always privileged private transport. Not by chance do nearly 300 million inhabitants consume around 50% of the gasoline produced in the world. Putting gasoline and gasoil together, the quantity

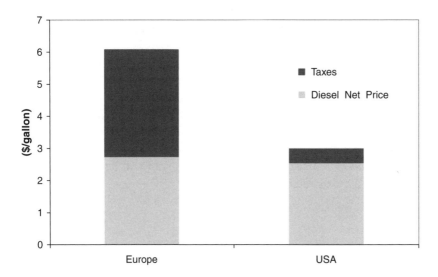

Figure 4.10   Tax burden on diesel fuel in 2010 (Europe and the USA)

Sources: U.S. Energy Information Administration, European Commission

reaches nearly 735 billion litres per year. Taxation on fuels provides the State with around $100 billion a year. This is clearly a political choice, based on certain principles typical of US culture, which has given positive results, in economic terms, during the years of low oil prices but is now showing its weaknesses.

Europe, on the other hand, has always assisted public transport in the cities as well as outside (e.g. metros, trains, ferries, buses etc.), demoting, generally speaking, the automobile to residual transport chores, tourism or individual comfort. The idea of taxing in punitive fashion individual transport by car started out from here.

In the various European countries, however, taxation on the automobile – and hence on fuels – is in some way aimed at supply of services of a certain level for the motoring citizen: a very efficient road network; well-maintained and safe roads; free, well-policed motorways; and car parks that are easy to use and with spaces available. Bicycle paths are also an integral part of the road system.

In certain European countries taxation on vehicles and fuels function as an additional component, but not openly declared as ordinary taxation. For example, in Italy, the revenue deriving from taxation on gasoline and diesel is around €35 billion per year, compared to the value of the goods taxed of about €20–25 billion. If we also add the taxes on other petroleum products, apart from gasoline and diesel fuel, the number arrives at €50 billion per year. This amount is updated continually since it is linked to the industrial price. As the oil companies' price list rises, the taxes increase automatically.

Just to give an idea of the size of this phenomenon in the European context, we may remember that while the volume of gasoline consumed in the USA is about 30 times greater than that in Italy, the tax revenue in America derived from automotive fuels is about three times lower than that in Italy. Obviously the situation is not very different in the other European countries.

Let us hope that a significant part of this sum will be used for investments for a more efficient transport policy.

5
World Oil Flow

Many of the distortions existing today in the world oil market stem from the loss of control of the processes started in past times to respond to a vision of economic rationalization.

When we note that the USA, while consuming over 22 million barrels per day of petroleum products, have created a refining capacity that can produce in continuous regime only about 14–15 million barrels per day, we can conclude that they decided to depend structurally on procurement of refined products coming from other geographic areas. The dependence of many industrialized nations on procurement of raw material (crude oil) from producing countries is often a necessity imposed by nature (oil is not found everywhere). However, dependence for finished products on other refining countries is an economic and strategic choice that provides benefits if well managed and monitored as time goes by, but that can also become a heavy burden if it slips out of control and becomes a strategic limitation. One often has the sensation that many choices in the oil field were made with a purely economic vision and, being based only on company ends, thus, short term by necessity. It is hard to discern any guidelines programmed by national authorities in a sector so strategic and decisive for the economy of a country.

To understand better what is happening today, we can look at some historic decisions made in the 1950s and 1960s by the leading US oil companies. We have to go back to a time when the price of crude at the origin, at the loading terminals in the various producing countries, was effectively fixed by the US multi-nationals (the famous Seven Sisters that Enrico Mattei talked about), and it was so low that the price at the final destination represented over 50% of the cost of transport. Reduction of transport costs was therefore a fundamental factor in the economic strategies of the US companies.

If we look at the movements of oil at that time (see Figure 5.1), we can clearly see that about 80% of the crude came from the Persian Gulf and reached the Atlantic basin via the Suez canal. The crude needed for the growing consumption in the USA, therefore, had to arrive first

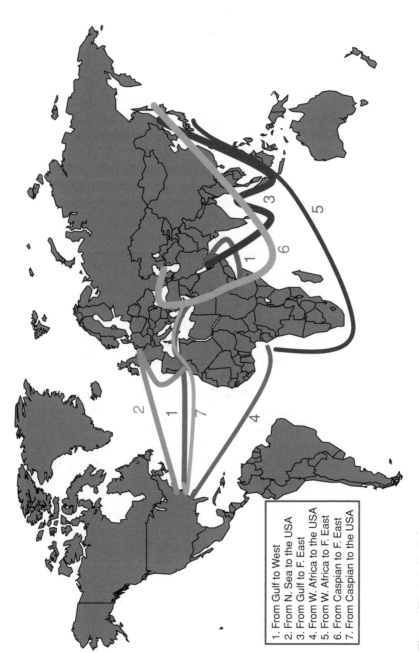

1. From Gulf to West
2. From N. Sea to the USA
3. From Gulf to F. East
4. From W. Africa to the USA
5. From W. Africa to F. East
6. From Caspian to F. East
7. From Caspian to the USA

Figure 5.1 World oil flow

in the Mediterranean and proceed accross the Atlantic, with very high transport costs.

Let us remember yet again that the USA did not require all the refined products obtainable from crude, but essentially just gasoline. Construction of further refineries to produce gasoline would have produced an excess of other products (gasoils, fuels) which would have to be exported and, thus, be re-transported with high additional costs. Europe too was going through a phase of economic boom due to post-war reconstruction and the industrialization of new areas. Europe needed fuels and electricity. It was possible to satisfy the needs of the two sides of the Atlantic with an integrated industrial plan, aiming to optimize everything; by building refineries in Europe that the US market needed, thus it became able:

• to produce and export gasoline to a privileged market, with good economic returns, providing availability of hard currency needed to pay for the raw material;
• to produce at marginal costs the fuel oil for the power stations being built, to provide energy for the expanding industrial system; and
• to develop the technology for diesel engines (little used in the USA) to use the gasoil produced and maximize export of gasoline.

This design made sense and offered secure economic returns. Therefore, the plan took shape and saw the massive construction of refineries in Italy (at the centre of the Mediterranean) and at Rotterdam, the key point for supply of gasoil to Germany. Furthermore it was essential to heavily promote the construction of power stations fed exclusively with fuel oil (a product considered as refinery waste), if possible located near the refineries. The newspapers of the time also tell us of the pressure exerted by the oil industry on the political world to reach its objectives.

This model worked perfectly until the end of the 1960s, but it was met with many difficulties that worsened with the first oil crises. Firstly, the closure of the Suez canal in June 1967. All the tankers from the Persian Gulf were forced to circumnavigate Africa to reach the Mediterranean, where the refineries were found. Clearly the economies on the transport costs completely disappeared. To take the crude, after the long circum-navigation of Africa, into the Mediterranean or to North Europe and then depart from there to take the gasoline to the USA, added extra costs as compared with the alternative voyage direct from the Persian Gulf towards the USA.

The system managed to resist, thanks to some adjustments to the transport element. The tankers that carried 60,000–80,000 tonnes of crude were replaced by supertankers carrying up to 350,000 tonnes. In this way the unit cost of transport was kept down and all continued as before. Furthermore, in the meantime, from 1973, OPEC took control of the prices and imposed a significant increase of around $10 per barrel. This took the transport cost to an acceptable fraction of the cost of crude at final destination.

Starting from 1973, two parallel processes got under way:

- Energy diversification in all the industrialized countries, tending essentially towards the production of electricity in an alternative way to that of the oil-fired power stations. In Europe, in the following decade, the demand for fuel oil fell to about 20% of the total oil demand.
- Construction of refineries in the producing countries, with the clear intention of shifting margins of the oil cycle from the companies towards the producing countries. These refineries were obviously oriented towards the export of finished products to international markets and they were built in those countries with huge financial resources (petrodollars) and with only a modest internal demand for petroleum products (Saudi Arabia, Kuwait).

TRANSFORMATIONS IN THE DOWNSTREAM

The result of all this was to create a very competitive market for finished products (the prices applied by the producing countries can be lower) and consequently, a reduction of the refining margins in all the plants with a relatively simple technological cycle; oriented towards production of fuels for power stations (no longer necessary) and marginal quantities of gasoline for export to the USA. A dramatic process of restructuring the refining system in the countries on both sides of the Atlantic started in the 1980s. All the refineries with a simple cycle that did not have a local pool of consumption (including adjacent power stations) were shut down. Those more modern and better located to supply the city outskirts or export gasoline to the USA were restructured with the installation of conversion plants. To illustrate this, Table 5.1 lists the closures in Italy, the European country necessarily most affected by this process, and in the USA, where the liberalization laws introduced by the Reagan administration accelerated the rationalization process.

Table 5.1 Italian refineries

Company	Location	Technology complexity	Status	Capacity 1973 [1000 bbl/day]	Capacity 2010 [1000 bbl/day]
AGIP Raffinazione	La Spezia	low	Closed	85	–
AGIP Raffinazione	Rho	high	Closed	80	–
ALMA	Ravenna	low		4	–
API	Falconara	mid		80	–
Aquila	Trieste	low	Closed	50	78
Arcola Petr.	La Spezia	low	Closed	20	–
ENI	Livorno	high		104	–
ENI	Porto Marghera	mid		90	108
ENI	Sannazaro	high		120	221
ENI	Taranto	mid		84	118
ERG	Genova	low	Closed	130	–
ERG	Melilli	mid		–	255
ERG	Priolo	high		300	250
Esso	Augusta	high		182	196
Gaeta IP	Gaeta	low	Closed	80	–
Italiana energia & servizi	Mantova	high		65	58
IPLOM	Busalla	low		32	38
Kuwait Petroleum	Naples	mid	Closed	130	–
Lombarda Petroli	Villasanta	low	Closed	22	–
Milazzo	Milazzo	high		400	280
Gela	Gela	high		90	129
Rome	Pantano	low		86	86
San Quirico	San Quirico	low	Closed	30	–
Saras	Sarroch	high		360	355
Sardoil	Porto Torres	low	Closed	90	–
Sarni	Bertonico	low	Closed	80	–
Sarom	Ravenne	low	Closed	140	–
Sarpom	Trecate	high		260	180
Tamoil	Cremona	mid		80	100
Volpiano	Volpiano	low	Closed	80	–

In the USA an even more extensive and drastic process took effect in two directions:

- Reduction of refining capacity with closure of uneconomic plants and concentration of ownership in the hands of fewer proprietors (Figure 5.2).
- Increase of the rate of utilization of existing capacity (higher operational efficiency) (Figure 5.3).

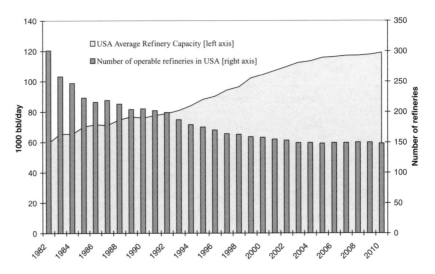

Figure 5.2   Number of refineries versus average refining capacity

Source: U.S. Energy Information Administration

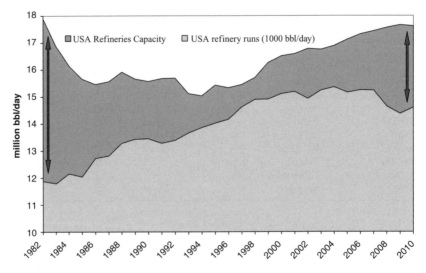

Figure 5.3   Refining capacity versus rate of utilization (USA)

Source: U.S. Energy Information Administration

In this context whatever plan there was for construction of new refineries was shelved. The last new refinery built in the USA dates back to 1976. In Italy too, the last refinery built was at Melilli (Siracusa) in 1976: since then, only upgrading work has been carried out on some existing plants.

All the tables of reference and the strategic lines of the past were wiped out and the oil industry began to live from one day to the next, incapable of making any overall plan to face the challenges of the future decades. In a situation of low prices and refining margins at the limits of survival, the companies limited themselves to closing each year with more or less positive results rather than make bets on the future. The continuation of this situation for over two decades created a survival culture in the oil downstream, which from that time has remained captive of a business philosophy tied to day-by-day dynamics; without realizing that the famous mole in the story was burrowing underground tunnels that would have provoked a crisis of capacity and lack of technology in the following decade.

This background explains the variations in the flow of crude supplies starting from the 1990s. To the prevalent direction of flow from East to West (Persian Gulf towards Europe and the Americas) an increasingly important flow towards the Far East was added. At the beginning this was low-quality, cheaper crude (the environment was not yet a relevant theme in the Far East), then the demand for light, low-sulphur crudes grew slowly. Refiners in the Far East turned their gaze on higher-quality crudes from the Gulf as well as from West Africa, triggering a commercial conflict with the US market, which hitherto had used them exclusively.

The arrival of Far Eastern operators in West Africa coincided with the rekindling of civil wars in many of the countries either already producing crude or with the potential to. This was obviously not an automatic coincidence, but certainly it would appear to be not unconnected with the events.

The history of the 2000s to date confirms that the consolidation of the processes of the previous decade and the new conflicts taking shape contributed towards directing world crude movements to the west or to the east. West Africa showed it was an area of bitter conflict and competition, where the game for control of crude oil was played on several fronts:

- political and military support in the local conflicts;
- massive assistance in building civil works, payment for which was expected to be made in crude oil in the future;
- partnerships for interventions in various business areas which could provide the country with some development also outside the oil sector.

Then the confrontation, perhaps even more bitter, in the Caspian Sea area came to the forefront. This area seems to have a potential for development comparable to that of the Persian Gulf. The area belongs to a series of member states of the ex-USSR and Iran. After the fragmentation of the USSR, the major oil companies raced to obtain mineral concessions in the area, with some clear-cut successes. From some years ago, however, the situation seems to have become a little more complicated because of the limitation of the export routes from the Caspian area towards the international markets, involving the need to resolve the following problems:

- Crossing Russian or Iranian territory.
- Reaching the Mediterranean without disturbing maritime traffic in the Dardanelles.
- Equipping the Mediterranean, historically an area importing oil, to export a mass of light crudes to more remunerative markets.

On this front the political, and sometimes military, reports inform us of growing tensions in the areas of transit, today or tomorrow, of the pipelines. The stakes in this game are very high and of strategic consequence: certainly beyond the scope of our present tale.

WORLD SUPPLY STRUCTURE

Another aspect of oil movements concerns the pinpointing of canals via which the crude, produced in various nations, reaches its final markets and how much of this crude contributes to support the dynamics of the oil market through commercial transactions. In the first place we should split world production into two distinct segments:

- that of the *guaranteed flows*, namely the part of world production that, every day, independently of the price level, is able to reach its final destination. This part represents about 88% of the production; and
- that of the *flows dependent on the price*, namely that part of the production that reaches any final market whatsoever only if its price is adequate and competitive. This part represents about 12% of the production.

It is interesting to look into the two segments defined above and shown in Figure 5.4, especially the one of the guaranteed flows, to understand the level of fragility of the physical markets for crude, where only a tiny fraction of the production is exchanged every day.

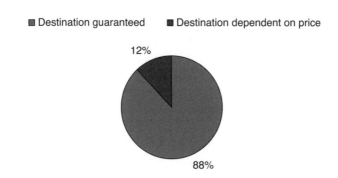

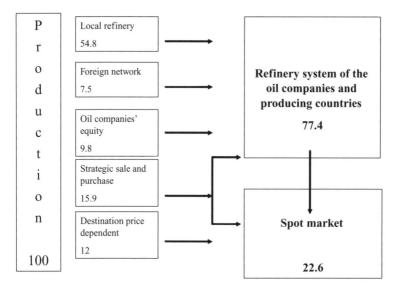

Figure 5.4   Destinations guaranteed and destinations dependent on the price

Therefore, in the oil market a gigantic space for manipulation is created. By moving only marginal quantities an enormous pressure can be exerted on the balance of the world market (such as the phenomenon of the squeeze on Brent).

In greater detail (as shown in Figure 5.5), we may note that:

• About 55% of the crude extracted by the producing countries is used in their internal refining system to cover their domestic needs. A small percentage of refined products (under 10%), in excess of the domestic requirement, is exported to other markets.

Figure 5.5   Destination of crude (%)

- About 7–8% of the crude is transferred to refining and distribution circuits that some producing countries own in the main areas of consumption (e.g. Saudi Arabia, Venezuela, Kuwait, Libya).
- About 10% represents the crude due to the oil companies for the repayment of their investments (the so-called equity quota) and which is sent either to their refining system or sold in the international markets.
- Some 15–16% of the production, historically, is destined by many countries to repay works and goods of strategic nature (e.g. major civil works, infrastructures and means of transport, military expenses).

Only 12% of world production is linked every day to spot or short-term sales contracts. This segment, plus other fractions of crude from the preceding segments, for a total never greater than 25%, constitutes the base of what we call the physical oil market. Out of a production of around 88 million barrels per day, the crude responding to commercial transactions does not exceed 20–25 million barrels per day.

From these data it is easy to see how the market forces do not affect the overall mass of demand and world oil supply but only a very limited segment in the hands of just a few operators. This fragile and critical balance is rocked today by the power of speculative finance which upsets the precarious equilibrium of what was formerly the international oil market.

6

The Classical Model of the International Oil Market

When analysts speak of the price of oil they are normally referring to the classical model of demand and supply. There is, however, a specific complexity in the technological model of the oil market, which when the model is applied *tout-court* leads to completely mistaken and paradoxical results. Not only are we unable to find an instrument that allows us to forecast the evolution of the price of oil (which any respectable model should do, at least in terms of revealing overall tendencies), but we cannot even manage to give a logical interpretation of events past and present. Many analysts in veneration of the model they use are forced to make far-fetched readings of the input data, so as to make them coherent with the facts of the market.

In the oil market there is only one incontrovertible fact, namely the evolution of the price of oil. Every day purchases and sales are completed on the basis of a price accepted by the buyer and the seller. On the basis of this figure physical transactions and payments take place. Price is therefore an incontrovertible fact. The price used one day differs from that of the day before or the day after. The reason for these variations is the mystery we need to unravel. The dynamics of demand and supply applied in the classical way are of little use. Let us try to see why.

When we examine the data regarding world oil demand and supply we normally refer to the International Energy Agency (IEA).

Table 6.1 is nothing more than the materialization of an interpretative model in which a forcible comparison of two dissimilar sets of data is made as if they were homogeneous and related to the same market dynamics we wish to understand. Actually, the comparison is made between:

- the world oil supply from the producing countries (OPEC and non-OPEC); and
- oil demand as the aggregate of finished products (e.g. gasoline, gasoil, fuel oil etc.).

Table 6.1 Global oil demand and supply

Global Oil Supply and Demand										(MB/D)
	2010					2011				
Source: IEA 18/01/2011	1 Q	2 Q	3 Q	4 Q	2010	1 Q	2 Q	3 Q	4 Q	2011
World Oil Demand	**86.3**	**86.9**	**88.6**	**88.9**	**87.7**	**88.6**	**88.4**	**89.8**	**89.7**	**89.1**
OECD	45.9	45.2	46.6	46.7	46.1	46.3	45.0	46.1	46.3	45.9
Non OECD	40.4	41.7	42.0	42.2	41.6	42.3	43.4	43.7	43.4	43.2
of Which ex FSU	4.2	4.1	4.4	4.3	4.3	4.4	4.2	4.5	4.4	4.4
World Oil Supply	**86.5**	**87.1**	**87.4**	**88.2**	**87.3**	**88.3**	**88.4**	**88.9**	**89.4**	**88.7**
Non OPEC Supply	52.4	52.8	52.8	53.3	52.8	53.1	53.1	53.5	53.9	53.4
OPEC Crude (X)	29.1	29.1	29.3	29.5	29.2	29.5	29.5	29.5	29.5	29.5
OPEC NGLs	5.1	5.2	5.4	5.5	5.3	5.7	5.8	5.9	6.0	5.8
Stock Change	**0.2**	**0.2**	**-1.2**	**-0.7**	**-0.4**	**-0.3**	**0.0**	**-0.9**	**-0.3**	**-0.4**

Source: International Energy Agency

From the figures we can deduce, at various times, the level of relative imbalance, namely, the excess or deficit of supply vis-à-vis demand. We are therefore able to estimate the effect on the available level of stocks among the sectors' market players (e.g. producers, refiners, distributors and transporters). Subsequently, an indication of the movement of the price of oil can be derived from the fluctuation of stocks levels. An increase of the stocks may project a fall in prices while a fall in stocks may forecast a rise in prices. In practice, however, the application of this model is of no help. The indications obtained are systematically contradicted by the market, which seems to obey other factors. The reason, apparently mysterious, does, on the contrary, follow a rigorous logic.

In Figure 6.1, covering the same quarterly periods starting from 2003, the variation in the level of stocks with the corresponding variation in the price of Brent are depicted. It is clear that in about 50% of the cases the formula

$$Price = f \, (supply - demand)$$

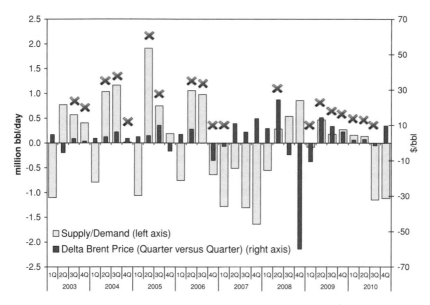

Figure 6.1 Variation of stocks versus variation in the Brent price

Source: International Energy Agency

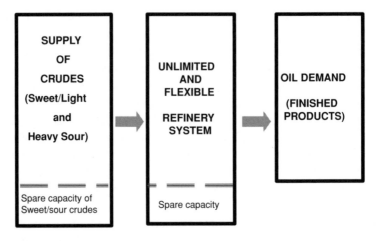

Figure 6.2   The classical model of demand/supply

does not provide any assistance. The crosses indicate each instance where the classical model of demand/supply is unable to explain the market rules. In fact, it is often that a rise in price corresponds erroneously to an increase in supply, when – on the contrary – economic theory tells us that the exact opposite should take place. The data for stocks are the final ones, published with around a year's delay vis-à-vis the market situation at the time. They are, thus, not influenced, as we shall see later, by the margin of error that exists due to uncertainties in the flow of data. Using the available data in each specific period, the correlation would be still unreliable.

The apparently mysterious reason for these results follows a simple and strict logic.

It has just been mentioned that the global model in practice compares two dissimilar elements, the supply of crude, that is, the raw material, with the demand for finished products (obtained by the refining process of the raw material). This is assuming that the world refining system is, on a daily basis, capable of transforming the raw material produced and sold by producing countries, into the array of finished products required by the market.

Figure 6.2 outlines the classical model for interpreting the encounter between demand and supply.

The classical model was amply justified and gave reasonable explanations for the movement of the market, as long as it was possible to make the following assumptions:

- The potential availability of raw material is always greater than the level of demand for finished products. In other words, there is always spare capacity in the productive system for processing high-quality light crudes as well as low-quality heavy crudes.
- The world refining system is characterized by spare capacity for the transforming units, whether they use simple or complex technology.

In actual fact, the structural changes in recent years have been such that both these hypotheses are no longer valid. The model of the world oil market has mutated into a new scheme (Figure 6.3) in which:

- the unused availability of raw material is limited exclusively to the availability of low-quality heavy crudes; and
- the spare capacity in the refining system has fallen drastically and is limited to a few plants of simple technology (where the possibility of obtaining high-quality gasoline from heavy crudes is very slender).

The change in productive systems has made it necessary to modify the interpretative models of the oil market. To continue to try to explain the market scene through the old models is simply useless. Even more is any attempt to make price forecasts using these models.

Yet, it is still the continuous and widespread practice of the major international analysts in using this model that, in the end, they are forced to deform the model's input data in a totally irrational way. To

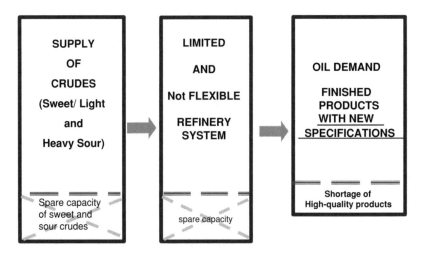

Figure 6.3   The modern supply/demand model

obtain the evolution of prices, data considered definitive and not subject to interpretation, as an output of the interpretative model, analysts are obliged to work on the input data, that is, on the movements of demand and supply. The unavailability of objective data in real time makes this manipulation of subjective estimates by analysts possible and hard to contest. It is, thus, possible to reconstruct the events of the recent past and above all to describe the present in an arbitrary way, particularly in such a way as to succeed in justifying, if used as an input of the model, the movement of price levels. If, for example, the price of oil has risen, on the basis of the model there can only have been a combination of a reduction in supply or an increase in demand.

Analysts, in the absence of available information, are often forced to derive their data through econometric models which allow them to be inferred. These are models which often have as their fundamental variable the sole irrefutable piece of data on the oil market, namely, the price of crude oil itself. They are, therefore, models of the type:

$$\text{Demand} = f\,(P\,\text{Brent})$$
$$\text{Supply} = f\,(P\,\text{Brent})$$

It is not difficult to imagine that such models can create vicious circles that often circulate in the market (see Figure 6.4). Rising prices generate forecasts of increasing demand and falling supply, and hence expectations of further rise in prices. These mechanisms thrive for what may be long periods, with sudden and unjustified collapses. But, above all, the tendency of analysts who make use of this model is to envisage the future as an exact copy of the present, with some insignificant cosmetic touches.

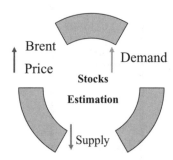

Figure 6.4   The vicious circle in the classical demand/supply model

Box 6.1   Variations in Estimated IEA Stocks

To illustrate this, Figure 6.5 shows an example of the adjustments made to the estimate of the yearly imbalance between demand and supply, concerning the same time period, in the course of the various updates as the confirmed data become available from time to time.

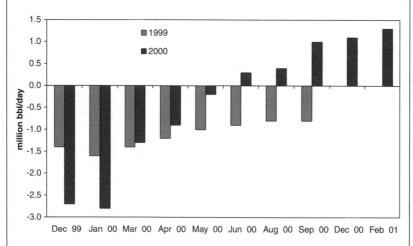

Figure 6.5   Adjustments to the estimate of the yearly imbalance between demand and supply

Source: International Energy Agency

It is important to spotlight these structural data, which are unfortunately still considered an irrelevant point of detail. Generally speaking, the classic market model derives its indications regarding the crude oil price trend on the basis of imbalances between demand and supply: under one million barrels per day. Such data are often the grounds for a violent debate on expectations for future months. But the error contained in the data under debate is far greater, 4/5 million barrels per day, than the stock imbalance, at most 1 million barrels per day. This analysis is what forecasts are based on.

We can certainly conclude that the global analysis and forecasts based on the classic models of demand and supply are only expressions of subjective opinions propped up by partial items of information lacking in objectivity. The problem of information in the oil market is very critical and features levels of transparency and availability that are very different, depending on the nature of the data in question:

- High level of transparency and availability in real time of prices and futures in the markets. The data can be accessed on line, minute by minute, from the various specialized sources.
- Partial level of transparency of the prices of physical transactions in crude oil. Much of this information, of a confidential nature since it concerns transactions between private parties, is estimated with varying levels of reliability by the specialized sources using particular criteria, accepted in oil industry practices.
- Medium level of reliability of the data concerning estimates of production in the main producing countries. The trustworthiness of the data is inversely proportional to the political control exercised over the level of oil production.
- Low level of reliability of the data regarding demand, with particular uncertainty between consumption and variation of the stocks of finished products in the various market areas. The only data available are those published monthly by the IEA, which itself either gathers them from the member countries (with average delays of 6–9 months), or estimates them for the non-member countries.

In particular, the uncertainties in estimates of demand and supply levels may arrive at quantities of 4 or 5 million barrels per day, as much as 5–7% of the total. We can certainly conclude that the analysis and forecasts based on the classical models of demand and supply at the global level are only expressions of subjective opinions propped up by partial items of information lacking in objectivity.

7

The Short-term Model of the International Oil Market

It is not easy to describe in detail how the oil market's model should be structured in such a way that it faithfully reflects the price dynamics as they relate to the fluctuations in the demand and supply balance. It is also necessary to take into account some essential features of the technological model of the oil industry together with the qualitative composition of both demand and supply. A functional model for industrial use can even contain over five thousand variables. In our case, we shall limit ourselves to the bare essentials, always trying, however, to identify the internal dynamics of the model and, thus, of the market itself.

For instructional purposes, we shall refer to the sketch of the model shown in Figure 7.1.

The sketch revisits the themes examined in the previous chapters, but describes in more detail – even if schematically – the segments of the oil cycle. In particular, the following points are considered:

- The supply of raw material, crude oil, is not just a homogeneous quantity, which can fluctuate with changes in production as decided by producing countries, but an aggregate of different qualities of crude extracted and put on the market. At least four families of crudes are on offer:
  - light crudes without sulphur (sweet light) – much sought after and specialized for production of high-quality products, both gasoline and gasoil;
  - light crudes with sulphur (sour light) – always sought after but which require additional refining processes to eliminate the sulphur (or other contaminating elements);
  - heavy crudes without sulphur (sweet heavy) – very useful for catalytic conversion processes (cracking plants); and
  - heavy crudes with sulphur and metals (sour heavy) – namely, the worst quality crudes that require vigorous refining and transforming processes to obtain marketable products.

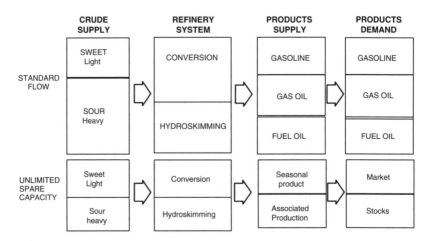

Figure 7.1 The classical industrial model

- The world refining system can be split into at least two large categories:
  - refineries with a high conversion level, where the hydrocarbon molecules undergo profound transformations and light products can be obtained even from the heavy fractions of the raw materials available; and
  - refineries with a simple cycle (hydroskimming), where the crude is subjected only to a distillation process, with treatment of the virgin naphtha at the reforming unit for production of a minimum amount of gasoline.
- The reference markets of the model are two in number:
  - the crude oil market, where refiners purchase crude from the producing countries and the oil companies; and
  - the finished products market, where the consumers (primary and secondary, namely simple citizens or industrial organizations) buy products from the refiners.
- In the crude oil market the price is the outcome of exchanges between producers and refiners, in the products market the price derives from the dynamics of the exchanges between consumers and refiners.
- The refiners represent the linkage between the two markets. Through the refining system the alignment or divergence of the two markets takes place. A model of the oil market which does not contain the description of the dynamics of the refining system is absolutely

inadequate for any representation, even the simplest one, of these markets.

- For a simplified representation we have considered the possibility of producing and marketing the three fundamental products in the marketplace, namely gasoline, gasoil and fuel oil.

We shall now see how the use of a model, even an extremely simplified one, but one which contains descriptions of the minimum variables, enables us to describe some of the phenomena regarding the distortions of the market. This has been witnessed in the last decade.

Let us give an example – theoretical for its level of simplification but sufficiently close to the phenomenology of the market. Suppose we are at the beginning of July, right in the middle of the gasoline season (the so-called driving season). Referring to the model just described, we have a situation in which:

- The producers of light crudes will have already committed their productive capacity and probably already sold their production of the summer months (July and August). Thus, there is no longer any additional availability of light crudes on the market.
- The refiners, who have already bought the crudes most suitable for gasoline production, have also programmed the maximum use of all the conversion plants, to produce the greatest volume of gasoline obtainable from those crudes in those plants. Thus, there is no additional capacity available for sophisticated refining.

Let us suppose that in this situation there is additional demand for gasoline and hence a substantial increase in its price. What can a refiner do to meet market needs and exploit a possibility to earn more? Certainly he will try to act with all the means he has at hand, namely:

- The refiner will go to the crude market to buy marginal additional quantities. But, seeing that there is no longer any availability of light crudes, he will be forced to buy volumes of heavy crudes, the only ones with some spare capacity, normally from producers in the Persian Gulf.
- He will have to process these crudes in the only plants that are not completely utilized in his refinery (which is already working at 100% with the most sophisticated plants to produce gasoline), namely the technologically simple plants (hydroskimming).
- From processing the heavy crudes purchased in the simple refining plants the refiner will get around 10% of gasoline and around 90%

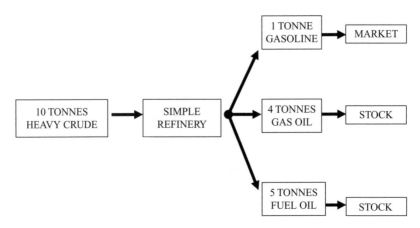

Figure 7.2   Refining cycle for a heavy crude to produce 1 tonne of gasoline

of other products (gasoil, fuel oil), which are high in sulphur content and are of very poor quality.

This means that to obtain a tonne of gasoline with this marginal cycle, our refiner has to buy and process about 10 tonnes of heavy crude, much more than he really needs (see Figure 7.2).

What impact will this marginal activity have on the market? Let us examine the main effects:

- The market will notice an increase in the demand for crude oil (raw material) nine times greater than the consumer market effectively needs, concentrated in the heavy crudes segment, whose relative price will rise in mid-summer (during the gasoline season), in total contra- diction to the normal expectations of industry professionals. In this season, one expects the light crudes to be the most expensive and sought after.
- The stocks of gas oil and fuel oil will increase (their production is linked to the processing of heavy crudes for the additional pro- duction of gasoline) and their price will fall. This will make the increase in price of heavy crudes, rich in fuel oil and gas oil, incomprehensible.

In conclusion, the market will have gasoline prices sky-high, gas oil and fuel oil prices low, but the price of heavy crudes, the raw material for production of fuel oil and gas oil, relatively higher. No classical model can provide an explanation.

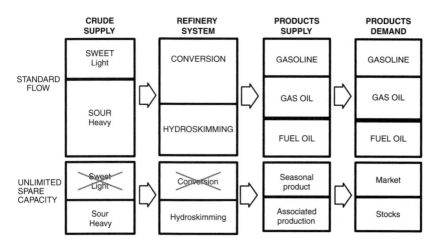

Figure 7.3   The modern oil industrial cycle

All this appears quite logical if we glance at the model illustrated in Figure 7.2 adapting it to the system in question, that is, a market without spare capacity for light crudes and without spare capacity for high-conversion refining plants (see Figure 7.3).

This type of model enables us to understand why the concept of seasonality has gone haywire as regards prices of petroleum products and qualities of crude.

The price peaks of the various products and the more specialized crudes for their production no longer take place regularly in the traditional season of maximum consumption, but in the phase when the productive system has the greatest difficulty to produce, for whatever reason (peak demand, plant production problem), the marginal quantity of an individual product.

Historically, the relative prices for petroleum products (formulated as indices vis-à-vis the unit value of the crude price) fluctuated in an orderly way during the various seasons of the year (see Figure 7.4):

- Gasoline started from winter levels of 1.2, to reach average levels of 1.4 in summer and fell to levels around 1.1 in late autumn.
- Gas oil, starting from levels of 1.3 in winter (above those of gasoline), could fall in late spring down to 1.0 (a level at which there was no sense in producing it, the finished product price being equal to the raw material price).
- Similar progressions can be found for the other products.

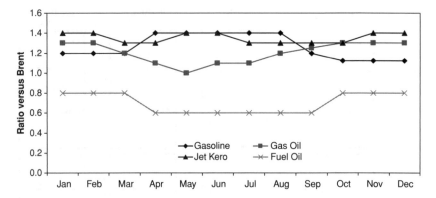

Figure 7.4   Relative prices of gasoline, gasoil, jet fuel and fuel oil

If we look at what happened, for example, during 2008 (see Figure 7.5), it is clear that:

- the price of jet fuel was continually above that of all other products;
- the price of gas oil was always above that of gasoline and had its relative maximum in May (1.28), well above the historic level of 1.0; and
- the gasoline price fell to its minimum level (1.07) both in July and November, without any apparent market logic.

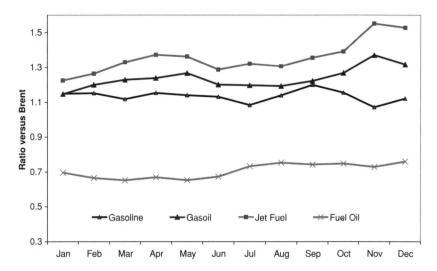

Figure 7.5   Relative prices of products in 2008

All this analysis demonstrates that in a market system in which the limits of the refining system create a decisive bottleneck, the price of crude is linked to the ones of the products. This is just the opposite of the assumption made in the classical model, where the fundamental role is attributed to the entry of raw materials in the crude oil market.

The crisis in the technological refining system has brought a new key factor in determining the level of petroleum prices: this is no longer a relationship between supply and demand of the raw material, but between high-quality finished products made available by the productive system and the level of demand for these same products in the various markets. The principle that the demand and supply relationship determines the price is, therefore, always valid, but it has to be applied to the correct relationship, namely to that regarding finished products. It is at this point that we see the narrowing between demand and supply, not at the raw material level. It is this technological aspect that usually escapes those analysts with a purely economic background. This is why, in the real world of the marketplace, the critical factors that determine prices are:

- the lack of US gasolines from March to August; and
- the lack of gasoil in Europe from October to February.

The balance within the international oil market at the various moments of the year hinges on these two variables. All the other factors are only a consequence, sometimes with an aesthetic effect, while at other times exercising a magnifying influence.

The role of finance has infiltrated these mechanisms and manipulated them in an exaggerated and speculative manner. Financial analysts, for their activities on the stock exchange, use algorithms based on statistic functions and they are, therefore, able to detect the repetition of cyclic phenomena, which every year, spanning a decade by now, are seen on the oil market. We are talking about a speculation that, in a free market regime, can in no way be stopped, at least until the current structural gap between productive systems and the level of demand for clean fuels is modified. Unfortunately, not only is there no plan for a solution on the horizon, but there is no sign yet of any awareness of the size of the problem.

Before ending this discussion on the structure of the current oil market model, we should clarify a fundamental concept. It's normal to affirm that speculative factors and unforeseen events in operational practice may make the use of the classical model based on supply and demand difficult, but that in the long run the dynamics of the fundamentals will prevail. This affirmation is certainly understandable making clear that short term corresponds to a period of time in which the bottlenecks of the industrial refining system will be overcome. In our case, we have seen that for nearly ten years we are in a systematic short-term context with the refining limits that we have already examined. Unfortunately, it is unclear when they can be removed from the scenario.

8

The Brent Market

Brent and the market for Brent have been mentioned several times. The features of this market will be outlined without going into technical specifics which concern the professionals. It will be explained why the adoption of Brent as a benchmark triggered a revolution that pushed both the producing countries and the oil companies out of the game regarding the control of the price of oil.

Brent is an offshore crude extracted off the Shetland Islands, part of the UK. It was the centre of one of the first oil strikes in the North Sea and certainly the most important, historically and politically. Shell UK, the field operator together with Exxon, gave the crude the name of a typical goose found in the region, namely the Brent goose. The discovery of Brent dates back to July 1971 but it was only on 13 December 1976 that the first oil tanker sailed from the loading terminal with a cargo of Brent crude. Initially, the production was exported from the offshore terminal of Spar, and subsequently, since November 1979, from the terminal of Sullum Voe. This terminal also receives, apart from Brent, Ninian, a crude discovered and extracted by the BP/Chevron consortium. In this way the exported crude became the Brent blend, which collected the production of around 15 fields in the North Sea operated by the two consortia, Shell UK-Exxon and BP-Chevron.

The Sullom Voe terminal, with its four jetties for export, allowed the simultaneous loading of four tankers of each type for whatever tonnage and size. It was the biggest and more flexible oil terminal of the time. It could handle whatever requirements of the customers, supplying wide flexibilities in loading dates. North European refiners could consider it almost an extension of their storage capacity and dispose of a cargo of Brent blend in 2–3 days.

Brent is considered a light sweet crude with its features of API (38 degrees) and sulphur content of 0.45%. The Blend crude is typically refined in North-West Europe and, by processing it, mainly gasoline and medium distillates are obtained. It soon became clear that Brent had no difficulties in competing with crudes of similar quality from OPEC countries like Nigeria, where the services are certainly poorer – so, for the same quality and price one would choose Brent.

The winning move, however, came in July 1986, when Shell UK, as the operator of Brent, decided to publish the 15 days Brent Contract. To understand what 'to publish a contract' means, and specifically for crude, some background information necessary to understand the mechanism involved will be provided.

THE SALE AND PURCHASE CONTRACT

We first have to explain what the structure of a purchase contract for a cargo of crude is. From the technical, commercial, administrative and legal standpoints, this is a very complicated document, and in order for it to be finalized, it needs the work of qualified international professionals. In fact, it is not enough to simply have financial resources and business acumen to enter the world of crude trading. A very specific professional competence is required. For the purpose of illustrating the complexity of the issues and hence the effects of the notable changes caused by Shell UK's introduction of the standard for Brent (15 days), we have briefly summarized the series of fundamental clauses that make up the structure of a contract in Box 8.1.

Box 8.1   The Principal Clauses in a Sale and Purchase Contract

The main clauses of a purchase contract for a cargo of crude oil are as follows:

1. *Detail of the Parties*: clear descriptions of the seller and the purchaser (name, address, company details).
2. *Grade*: descriptions of the essential features of the crude oil/object of the transaction, not to allow any ambiguity.
3. *Quantity*: the exact definition of the size of the cargo in terms of barrels and indication of the flexibility guaranteed at the moment of loading, namely the possibility that the ship is loaded with more or fewer barrels than the quantity envisaged in the contract. Normally, the purchaser may request a variation of +/− 5%, but he can obtain this only if the terminal operator agrees.
4. *Delivery*: defines the conditions and manner with which the seller delivers the crude to the purchaser (Incoterms), such as:

- FOB (FREE ON BOARD): the purchaser receives the crude at the terminal where he must present himself with his ship on the agreed day, and he becomes *immediately its owner*. This defines the classic purchase model for goods, when the purchaser enters the seller's shop, buys, pays, becomes owner and takes away the goods purchased;
- CFR (COST AND FREIGHT): the seller arranges on behalf of the purchaser the transport of the crude from the loading terminal until the point of delivery, obviously passing on the pertinent costs. The title of the goods transported is of the buyer. Here too we may refer to the model of a shop, where the purchaser buys, pays, becomes owner (for example, of a movable object) and requests the seller to arrange the transport (paid apart) to his own residence;
- CIF (COST, INSURANCE AND FREIGHT): as in the previous case, but with the addition of the insurance for the value of the cargo transported. We may refer to the previous example, where an insurance policy is requested against damage suffered during transport;
- DES (DELIVERED EX SHIP): the seller, whether he has not yet found a buyer or whether he wants to wait before selling, loads the crude on a ship and tries to sell it during the voyage. Obviously, delivery takes place at destination, likewise for the transfer of ownership. An example from everyday life could be that of the itinerant salesman who travels around with his goods which he owns, and meets the purchaser on his front doorstep.

5. *Price*: the formula for calculating the price of the cargo must be described unequivocally, indicating:
   - the reference benchmark (Arabian light, Brent)
   - the days considered for calculating the average value of the benchmark (the pricing period, that is the average of the month of loading, 5 days around the loading date), the price difference to apply to the benchmark (premium or discount) for the specific crude/object of the contract, automatic price adjustments in case of variation in the quality of the crude delivered vis-à-vis the contractual standard.

6. *Invoicing Quantity*: the seller's invoice must show the quantity that will be advised by the operator in the official document that accompanies the cargo, the so-called *Bill of Lading* (B/L). The

purchaser will be required to effect payment on the basis of this quantity. In case of dispute, the purchaser may complain but cannot reduce the amount of the payment.

7. *Payment*: in the oil industry, this clause is sufficiently standardized and envisages that the payment:
   - must correspond exactly with the clauses of price and quantity, without any discount, deduction or compensation for any reason whatsoever;
   - it's normally effected in USD;
   - must take place by telegraphic transfer available to the seller on the same day;
   - must be effected within 30 days, as of the date of issue of the Bill of Lading;
   - after the buyer receives a commercial invoice and the original copy of the B/L or an LOI (Letter of Indemnity).

   The clause also defines other aspects, such as:
   - the opening of a letter of credit (or other documents of credit) by the purchaser, before loading;
   - what to do if the day of payment falls on a day when the banking system is closed (payment due the day before or after such closure);
   - how to compensate the seller in case of delayed payment: normally payment of interest (at 2% above LIBOR) is required.

8. *Property and Risk*: as defined in the delivery clause, the time and place where the transfer of property takes place and consequently every risk that is passed to the owner will be specified (loss of cargo, pollution of the surrounding environment).

9. *Independent Inspection*: both contracting parties are entitled to appoint an independent inspector who can superintend all the loading operations and certify the quantity and quality of the cargo. Normally the parties agree on the name of the inspector and share the costs.

10. *Tankship Nomination*: the owner of the cargo (buyer or seller, depending on the delivery conditions) must:
    - arrange and ensure the arrival of a ship at the loading terminal at the date envisaged for loading, advising in good time the name of the ship;
    - advise the terminal operator at least 72 hours before and subsequently updating the estimate 48 hours and 24 hours before

the date and hour of arrival of the ship at the terminal (ETA =
Expected Time of Arrival);

- advise the terminal operator who to contact regarding any
operational action to be taken;
- be certain that the owner of the chartered ship is a member of the
ITOPF (International Tanker Owners Pollution Federation Ltd),
so as to give the terminal every guarantee in case of accident
and pollution, and ensure respect of all the international norms
regarding insurance, transport of alcohol and drugs, as well as
safety and maintenance.

In the absence of these requisites the access of the ship to the
terminal may be refused.

11. *Confidentiality*: all the information contained in a commercial oil
contract is strictly confidential between the parties and cannot be
divulged to anyone without the prior approval of the other party.
The only exceptions envisaged are:

- in cases of legal disputes and limited to that specific use;
- in cases of specific request by the tax authorities of the country
of the seller/producer of the crude.

12. *Measurement and Claims*: this clause sets out the rules in force at
the terminal, the measuring systems to be used and the procedures
to adopt in case of claims made by the purchaser in instances
of non-conformity with the standards prescribed by the contract,
including appeal to an independent inspector.

13. *Laytime*: this defines the number of hours available to the terminal
to load a ship of given size.

14. *Demurrage*: for any time exceeding that allowed for loading, the
compensation for the purchaser (who has to await the ship for
longer than planned) is established.

15. *Governing Law and Jurisdiction*: one of the key clauses in an
international contract is the definition of the jurisdiction to refer
to and the law to be applied. Normally in oil contracts reference
is made to English law.

It is also necessary to state whether, in case of dispute, arbi-
tration or the High Court will be submitted to, and to agree on
which one.

16. *Force Majeure*: this clause defines the list of all the exceptional
events deemed sufficient to suspend the obligations of the contracting parties (for example, interruption of production in the

oilfield and therefore the impossibility for the seller to deliver the cargo, documented breakdown of the ship and impossibility to reach the terminal in good time).
17. *Letter of Indemnity*: this states that in case of loss or delay of the Bill of Lading, before payment, the buyer must receive the letter of indemnity which can replace the original documents while they are being searched for or re-issued.
18. *Assignment*: the parties can assign the ongoing contract to another subject (affiliated or otherwise) who will assume all the obligations and rights deriving from the contract itself.
19. *Liability*: this defines the terms and limits of criminal and civil responsibility of the parties.
20. Other clauses.
21. *Contact* addresses of seller and buyer.

As can be clearly seen, to finalize a purchase contract for a cargo of crude oil is a very delicate and complex matter requiring very specific professional competences.

THE FORWARD MARKET FOR BRENT (15 DAY BRENT CONTRACT)

The revolution introduced by Shell UK consisted of the total standardization of the purchase and sale contract for a cargo of Brent crude. All the clauses had already been defined in detail and could not be either re-negotiated or modified. Anyone who wanted to buy or sell a cargo of Brent blend only had to use the standard contract, without getting involved in any of the complicated legal and administrative aspects of the commercial negotiation.

The only items to state in the contractual document were:

- names of the contracting parties, seller and buyer; and
- purchase price per barrel.

As already mentioned, for all the other clauses, reference was made to the standard contract published by Shell UK. In particular, the standardizations concerned:

- the quantity, fixed at 500,000 barrels for each cargo; and
- the acceptance date of the cargo by the buyer, namely 15 days before the loading date, hence the name given to the contract: 15 days Brent.

It was moreover to buy and sell cargoes of Brent which were to be produced and delivered in the following six months. This simplification of the negotiating process immediately amplified the possibilities of taking part in the business, even for those not strictly linked to the oil and related markets. Anyone with financial resources and a certain feel for the oil market (perhaps with the help of a qualified consultant) could enter the Brent market game. It was not yet the petroleum exchange and the pure financial market, but this was the first splinter from the historic confines of the petroleum elite.

Box 8.2   The Daisy Chain

Let us try to explain the mechanism of the 15 day Brent market with an example.

Suppose we are in January with the Brent market rather weak (as happened in 2009) and above all with prospects that are even more negative. A trader (B) decides to bet on a market recovery in April. He tries then, in January, to buy a cargo of Brent for the month of April. He believes that, amid the general pessimism, he will be able to buy in January the April cargo at a lower price than he would be able to buy in the future. He goes into the marketplace and tries to find someone who will sell him an April cargo. Suppose the going price for Brent on 18 January (the day when he entered the market) was $45 per barrel and for an April cargo his seller (A) asks for a price of $43 per barrel.

Suppose now that (A) and (B) close the deal in the morning of 18 January and that, later the same day, something happens (such as a burst pipeline in the Middle East, new maintenance programmes in the North Sea production fields) which causes an immediate rise in prices. Trader (B) sees that the April cargo, which he had bought at 10:00 a.m. for $43 per barrel, by mid-day, only two hours later, is worth $47 per barrel and he thus decides to sell it to (C) who in competition with others has already offered him as much as $47.50 per barrel. He has registered a profit of $4.50 per barrel, just with two phone calls (and a good understanding of the market).

These deals, which began on 18 January for a specific April cargo, can continue almost to the infinite, up to a certain date in March. We are describing the creation of a chain of transactions inside which hundreds of different subjects can participate. It may even happen that the same cargo passes through the hands of the same subject several times. If we try to draw on a sheet of paper the succession of transactions inside the same chain, with the passage of the cargo into the hands of the same subject, then we shall see that the sketch recalls the petals of a daisy. It is for this reason that the chains are known as daisy chains in petroleum slang. Naturally we are referring to what happens for one cargo, but every day the chains behind these transactions are dozens and dozens for each of the six months following the current one (in our example of January, all the cargoes up to the month of July in the same year can be negotiated). It is clear that every day, starting from a single physical cargo of Brent that will be available on a certain date as yet unknown, a number of cargoes of Brent will be bought and sold, simply on paper, with contracts that will not give rise, almost certainly, to the physical delivery of all the barrels effectively exchanged.

In our example, (B) has on the same day bought from (A) and sold to (C), earning $4.50 per barrel, without receiving or delivering any cargo of crude. The aggregate of the transactions can reach an enormous amount. For this specific market of 15 days Brent, peaks of dealings have reached around 50 million barrels per day, in contrast with a physical production of Brent blend of 700,000 barrels per day in the good times. Today the field produces only 200,000 barrels per day – 15 days Brent contract has a volume of business 70 times greater than its physical production.

Now the strategic objectives of the creation of the 15 days Brent contract become clearer:

- Creation of a benchmark whose apparent production, in terms of daily trading volume, was by far greater than any other benchmark proposed and applied by OPEC.
- Make available a benchmark beyond OPEC's control, supervised and regulated to a large extent by the oil companies that produced Brent.

Box 8.3   15 day Brent Contract

Let us return again to the previous example. The chain was formed on 18 January and up to March had involved thousands of subjects within itself.

It is clear that at a certain point, the April cargo, the subject of the deals between all these traders, will materialize and someone will have to take his ship to the terminal at Sullom Voe and collect the cargo. If the person who has to collect the cargo is a refiner, there will be no problem. If, however, the cargo finishes up in the hands of someone who entered the chain just to speculate, then there will be a problem to resolve. This person will have to handle the placing of the cargo in the market and find a refiner who needs it (obviously at a suitable price).

Let us see how the process of assigning a specific physical cargo to a person in the chain operates. We refer to the historic procedure, the one that gave origin to the name 15 days Brent. Recently some changes have been introduced and we shall examine them later.

For clarity we refer to the April cargo. On 13 March, BP, the terminal operator at Sullom Voe, will publish the programme of all the cargoes to be lifted during the month of April. This means that for each separate cargo (in all about 25 cargoes) the following are made known:

- the loading date; and
- the name of the producer (BP, Shell UK, Exxon, Chevron), owner of the cargo as a mineral right. Obviously each of these cargoes has been sold to other purchasers through the 15 days contracts.

Once the lifting programme has been published, the owner of each separate cargo must, 15 days before the estimated loading date, advise the terminal operator that he accepts the obligations (nomination of the cargo) and guarantees the dispatch of a ship in good time to collect the cargo. As previously explained, the obligation to nominate the cargo 15 days before the loading date has given this contract the name of 15 days Brent. But who is the owner of the cargo of Brent that will load, for example, on 5 April? Pinpointing the owner takes place with a particular mechanism. The mineral partner, the first owner of the cargo (as published by the operator) will telephone the person to whom the cargo was sold, passing on to him the obligation to nominate the cargo to the operator. The telephone used must be totally and exclusively dedicated to this service. It must never happen that a participant in the chain does not answer a call. Moreover, this telephone is connected to the services of British Telecom, who records and informs the exact time of the calls.

Every person who receives a call must decide whether to accept the nomination or pass it on to the next person in the chain. Clearly all those who entered the chain for speculative purposes will try to exit quickly, passing the nomination along to their purchaser.

If we consider the number of those in the chain, the number of telephone calls could go ahead *ad infinitum*. But there is a limit set by the conditions of the contract. The person who receives the nomination by 17:00 hours London time and does not succeed in passing it on to the successive trader or purchaser always before 17:00 hours London time, is obliged to nominate the cargo. If this person has suffered the nomination, in slang he is said to have been 'five o'clocked'.

Once the physical cargo is assigned to a person in the chain, all the other participants must, in any case, settle their commitments. This means that the person who takes the physical cargo must, however, purchase a paper cargo (of the same month) to deliver to the person after him in the chain. The natural solution of the mechanism would be for the physical cargo to go to the last person in the chain. But this rarely happens.

The market in which the physical cargoes of Brent are traded, whose loading date is already known, is called the Brent Dated Market. This price, published by specialized sources, establishes on a daily basis, the market reference since the time when Brent became used as benchmark. Participation in the 15 day Brent therefore offers the risk that, statistically, one may become the owner of a physical cargo of crude that must be handled, something that is certainly not easy for anyone who is not a producing company or a consumer of crude.

Box 8.4   The Price Risk in the 15 day Brent Contract

The example we have seen, an April cargo bought in January, is useful to comprehend the size of the potential risk for one who speculates with this contract.

We supposed that (B) bought the April cargo at $43 per barrel from (A) and sold it to (C) at $47.50 per barrel. Suppose now that (B) is the 'five o'clocked' trader, obliged to nominate the cargo and market it on the physical crude market. If for some reason the April market has crashed to $20 per barrel, our trader (B) will be forced to sell at $20 per barrel what he bought at $43 per barrel, risking an enormous loss. Furthermore, he will be obliged to buy a paper cargo for his purchaser (C).

This is exactly what happened on the London market in 1987, with the famous 'blood bath'. Many traders, facing certain bankruptcy, preferred to refuse the nominations and abandon the activity.

In these cases, the Brent producers (BP, Shell UK, Exxon and Chevron) had to take the place of the traders who were missing in the chain and take responsibility for the collection of the so-called distressed cargoes. These occurrences showed that Brent forward, another name for 15 days Brent, was not a perfect financial instrument, both because it showed it was not able to censure the functioning of the mechanism in cases of crisis with big falls in price levels, and because it limited the number of participants to those who could:

- shoulder financial commitments at least equal to the value of a cargo of 500,000 barrels;
- guarantee the handling of a physical cargo should the need arise; and
- honour their commitments in every market situation.

For these reasons, those participating in the Brent game, although numerous, could be considered as qualified members of an exclusive club. Structurally, however, it was regarded that the system's fragility was elevated at the moment when a forward contract for paper crude became a physical contract for Brent crude. This step in the chain's mechanism could become 'traumatic' creating anomalies in the system and substantially modifying price levels.

With some similarities to other markets, which we hope will not take offence, one could assert that the 15 days Brent constituted a market *d'elite*, a sort of high fashion *atelier* of the oil market, where:

- every contract was between two parties identified with names and surnames;
- the price was the outcome of free negotiations between these two parties; and
- a high-level professional and financial profile was required of the participants.

It became clear that the objective of a totally liquid and transparent market, with a daily trading volume equal to at least the oil production of the globe, had not been achieved. Yet, the creation of this benchmark has, in terms of dimensions and flexibility, outclassed the old Arabian Light crude.

THE IPE BRENT MARKET

What was needed was a mass-market Brent, a supermarket type Brent, an off-the-peg for the oil market. With this intent, in 1988 a new Brent market, purely financial, of a stock exchange type was created – the International Petroleum Exchange, IPE.

The features of this market were and continue to be:

- Nominal cargo (lot) reduced to 1000 barrels (no longer 500,000 barrels), a size which, at the prevailing prices, made it comparable to the value of similar financial operations on the stock exchange, such as the purchase or sale of company shares. It is a much more popular size, one that allowed the grocer or the barber (as one used to say) to get involved in the dynamics of the oil market, to have an opinion about OPEC and to feel him or herself adequately informed after reading the news.
- No delivery of physical oil was possible or envisaged (except for one precise case, more theoretical than practical). In this way, the critical and fragile passage, inherent in the 15 days Brent, was eliminated from the paper contract at the nomination of the physical cargo. Anyone could play around in this market without running the risk, one fine day at 5:00 p.m., of hearing that they had become the owner of a physical cargo of crude which had to be handled.
- The transactions no longer took place between single parties, a buyer and a seller, but between any party whatsoever and a clearing house (the Exchange). It was like going to the supermarket, a particular supermarket where one could buy and sell products, but where the price was not negotiated, but only read, made known on an electronic screen second by second with the fluctuation of purchases and sales.
- Every trader could sell or buy short what he or she did not yet possess. Every operation conducted on this market had to be closed within a certain time, as with the stock market. One could buy a lot of crude on day five, when the price was, for example, $50 per barrel, and resell it on day seven, when the price had become $52 per barrel. Or vice versa one could sell a cargo at $52 per barrel and re-buy it when the price was lower.

It was precisely here that the revolution in the international oil market took place. This market had no longer any connection with the physical crude oil market opening it up to the participation of any person capable of investing through normal banking channels, just as one does in the stock market. It was initially the oil markets' institutional bodies, companies, trading houses and banks acting on their clients' behalf that turned their attention to this new financial product. At a certain point, particularly after the start of the 21st century, when the market's volatility reached very high levels, thus, allowing those who traded in the market to make enormous profits, the main protagonists then became the banks and financial institutions who together with various US and international funds, started to operate the market as a pure financial venture, totally independent of the dynamics of the oil market.

Enormous movements of capital were seen, thousands of billions of dollars were rapidly shifted from various commodities and from the stock market towards the financial market of Brent, causing the price to rise, or fall, in the case of operations in the other direction. Price variations of $2–5 per barrel in one day became normal. This in itself became a big incentive for other parties to enter the business. So, at one point, a kind of fever enveloped the banks to hire experts in oil trading (poaching them from oil companies) to start and develop this business.

Quite clearly, we are talking about Brent, but we could extend all the concepts discussed to the analogous NYMEX market, the petroleum exchange of New York, where the WTI (West Texas Intermediate), the other crude comparable to Brent, is traded.

OPEC's decision to use Brent as a benchmark came soon after the birth of this market, effectively handing over total control of the oil price to international finance. Not everyone understood immediately the extent and consequences of what happened in 1988. There were many misunderstandings and perhaps the lack of a full perception of the mechanics of the commodity and stock exchanges in the decision adopted by OPEC. From the documents of the time and the declarations of the main players, it stands out clearly that the wish of OPEC was to link its crude prices to that of physical Brent crude in offshore UK, thus, pressuring that government to force it to negotiate its level of production.

One presumed a new edition of the price war that was declared two years earlier by Sheikh Yamani. No-one understood that a financial indicator was being adopted as a benchmark, outside the control of the UK government and the companies producing Brent. It was an easy mistake to make as the chosen benchmark was the value of Brent Dated, which officially represented the price of physical cargoes of Brent whose loading date was already known.

The price of a physical cargo sold by one party in the chain (perhaps forced by circumstances to nominate the cargo) to a refiner is normally not known. Neither of the two parties that sign a contract for Brent wishes to inform the market of the damage suffered or the advantage obtained and, thus, the value published by the sources is simply estimated on the basis of the indications coming from the parallel financial market of that day. Likewise, once the Brent IPE market was developed, it became a fact that dealings on the 15 days Brent market were influenced by what was read on the electronic screen of the Brent exchange. It therefore came about that the value of the financial Brent IPE generated all the other intermediate values that lead to the price of all the physical cargoes of crude sold in the world. Brent IPE generates the Brent 15 days, from which Brent Dated is derived, which in its turn is the basis for setting the price for all the crudes of the world.

THE DIVORCE BETWEEN OIL PRICE AND OIL

This bond was made official and duly sanctified by the decisions taken in 2002 by Saudi Arabia and Iran not to refer to the value of Brent Dated to set the price for their crudes, but rather to directly use the Brent IPE. They wanted to eliminate the intermediate step in the assessment of the value of Brent Dated by the specialized sources, whom they accused of being insufficiently neutral. It was in this new context that the divorce between the oil price and oil itself came about.

Let us suppose that on one fine day, because of financial operations by hedge funds, there was a massive purchase in the exchange of Brent contracts and that its price went up several dollars per barrel. That same day, the price variation would be reflected along the entire chain of the various types of Brent; the Brent 15 days and the Brent Dated. Consequently, this would have an impact on all crudes sold which use it as benchmark. If an analyst tried to relate the variation in the Brent price on that particular day to changes in the dynamics of offer and supply of crude, he would need a flight of fantasy to imagine events and their impossible and illusory correlations. The only link remaining between the financial markets of Brent and the physical one for crude is that of a certain sharing between financial professionals and oil traders of the market analyses as published by specialized firms. It should be noted that the studies and analyses published by the research departments of various international banks involved in this business have become predominant in recent times. The remarkable rise in the price of Brent to $147 per barrel in July 2008 was preceded by a series of analyses published by Merrill Lynch and other banks, which predicted (influencing the market?) an escalation of the price up to $250 per barrel.

As from May 2000, the ICE platform (Intercontinental Exchange) was created, and this subsequently assimilated the IPE and other institutions present in the sector. The scope was to create a sole platform that would allow professionals all over the world the opportunity to operate online in the oil futures markets, 24 hours a day.

9

Principal Uses of the Forward and Futures Markets

The two markets, 15 days Brent and the financial ICE, have continued to co-exist, simultaneously working in the price setting process, whilst still responding to the different needs of traders.

TAX SPINNING

The first activity of the crude oil producers of the United Kingdom was to optimize the taxation burden (tax spinning). The taxes due to the department of Inland Revenue were set as a fixed percentage (40–50%) of the value of each single cargo. The lower the price, the lower the taxes to be paid. The price had to be advised by each producer within 48 hours from completion of loading. This allowed the producing companies, in the two days following the loading, to intensify their trading operations on physical cargoes, and to attribute the lowest of the prices obtained to the cargo just taken and to declare it to the Inland Revenue with evident and sizeable tax advantages. This practice was tolerated by the British authorities, as a form of incentive to invest in offshore activities. Recent years have, however, seen limitations and restrictions being gradually imposed on this tax flexibility, forcing companies operating in the UK to pay taxes corresponding to the prices actually obtained.

BENCHMARKING

Brent Dated has been and continues to be used as the benchmark for more than 60% of the crudes sold worldwide (look back to Figure 3.2 which shows the price of crude with reference to the benchmark). All the crudes linked directly to Brent were valued by establishing a differential vis-à-vis the assessment as published in Platts on a given day.

For example, on 20 July a cargo of Bonny Light (a Nigerian crude) is valued on the market as Dated Brent + $1.50 per barrel. The valuation

Table 9.1 Correlation index between Brent and other international crudes

Crude	Origin	Correlation
Es Sider	Libya	1.000
Suez	Egypt	0.995
Escravos	Nigeria	0.998
Ekofisk	North Sea	0.995
Ural	Khazakstan	0.997
Kirkuk	Iraq	0.995
Cabinda	Angola	0.996
Iranian Light SK	Iran	0.986

Source: eprm

of the crude for that day, 20 July, will reflect the value of Brent of that day plus $1.50 per barrel. That is, if Brent stands at $75.00, the value of the cargo of Bonny Light will be $76.50 per barrel.

Table 9.1 shows the index of correlation between Brent and crudes from around the world since 1990.

One can understand how the assessment process affected by the specialized sources may represent a critical element in defining the value of a crude and, thus, the oil revenues of each single producing country. The main sources of information, Platts, Argus, LOR and Reuters, are continuously criticized by the producing countries for their activities being slanted towards protecting the interests of the oil companies. To avoid repeated discussions on the matter, in defining the value of Brent it is often preferred to cite the average of the values published by the various sources, so as to depend less on the personal views of the analyst who made that assessment.

HEDGING THE PRICE RISKS

A separate chapter is dedicated to describing the main activity that was made possible by the introduction of the Brent market, and which turned out to be the Trojan horse of the financial world to take, by storm, the oil market and break the power of the historical leaders, the producing countries and oil companies. This is the so-called hedging, in other words coverage of price risks.

After the international events that took place towards the end of the 1970s, we have seen how price volatility created conditions of total uncertainty for oil company operations, both in the short (procurement for the refining system, level of stocks) and long term (investments in the borderline areas whose production costs are higher). The Brent market, already in its first form, the 15 days Brent, but certainly much more so with its purely financial form as in Brent ICE, offered and continues to offer a way to eliminate or significantly limit the risks of oil professionals. The financial managers of these activities presented themselves, at quite acceptable costs, to their oil company contacts as insurers against the risk of price fluctuations. They were very successful in this role, building up a colossal business, which in the long run has completely inverted the roles played by everyone. Finance has become the fundamental business, the core business, with oil becoming a non-essential marginal incident.

A few examples will be given, quite simple and straightforward, to allow the reader who is not familiar with these operations to dip his or her toes into the world of financial hedging and the speculative activities linked to this sector.

Box 9.1   First Example of Hedging

As a first example let us take the case illustrated in Figure 9.1 below:

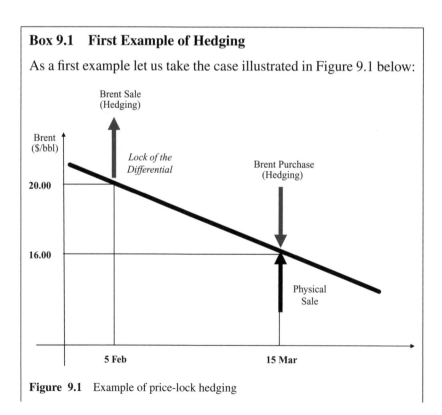

Figure 9.1   Example of price-lock hedging

Let us suppose that on 5 February an oil company, producer of a certain quality of Nigerian crude (e.g. Nigerian Brass River), is informed by the export terminal operator, that it must lift a cargo of 1 million barrels of Brass River on the coming 15 March. Obviously, since the company in question is a partner in the joint venture that produces the Brass River crude, the delivery of this cargo corresponds to its production quota, so that it can recover its investments in that month. The company must therefore lift the crude at the terminal and try to sell it in the market at the highest possible price so as to maximize its profit. As soon as he is contacted by the terminal operator, the commercial manager of the oil company puts his sales strategy into effect. Referring to our example, in order to make his decisions, he will make two assumptions:

- The crude price on 5 February is $20 per barrel.
- Market sentiment for the following weeks is very negative and there may be a significant fall in prices. Therefore, there is a real risk that the price on 15 March (estimated loading date) will be lower than that of 5 February.

The commercial manager will, therefore, try to sell his cargo of crude as soon as possible, perhaps trying to freeze today's price. Obviously the potential buyer has the same information and will hence try to do the exact opposite. Moreover, it is common practice in the oil industry that the price of a cargo is established on the basis of the market values on the day of loading, therefore, in our example, on the basis of the value ruling on 15 March. In the end, the cargo will be sold at the standard market conditions and accepted by the purchaser, namely at the price of Brent Dated ruling on 15 March, which no one knows. The negotiation is concluded (deal done).

But our commercial manager does not resign himself to suffering the uncertainties of the market for the more than 30 days wait until the loading date. He decides to enter the paper Brent market.

The same day, 5 February, in which he has sold his cargo of 1 million barrels of Brass River, he also sells 1 million barrels of Brent futures (short, he does not have them yet). Please note that in order to simplify the example, we assumed the hedging costs to be nil.

In practice, in the same day he has effected two commercial operations:

1. He has taken a contractual commitment to sell one cargo of Brass River which will load on 15 March, at the price of Brent ruling in the market on 15 March.
2. He has effectively sold (on the petroleum exchange) 1 million barrels equivalent of Brent at the price ruling on 5 February.

At this point he can only await the market outcome.

Let us suppose that, for once, the market forecasts are correct and, therefore, the crude price falls in the following weeks to reach $16 per barrel on 15 March. That same day the purchaser's ship presents itself at the terminal and loads 1 million barrels of Brass River. Obviously, the purchaser has paid the agreed price, that is, that of Brent at 15 March, namely $16 per barrel, with an overall outlay of $16 million. At the same time, our man decides to close his position with the petroleum exchange, buying exactly 1 million barrels of Brent today (the same quantity as that sold short on 5 February), at today's price of $16 per barrel. Having completed all his commercial transactions built around this cargo of Brass River, the commercial manager summarizes the situation:

	million dollars
1. Sale of 1 million barrels of Brent ($20/b)	+20
Hedging costs	
2. Purchase of 1 million barrels of Brent ($16/b)	−16
3. Sale of 1 million barrels of Brent ($16/b)	+16
Overall result obtained	+20

Our man, through the integrated deals done in the petroleum exchange in the Brent market, has cashed in 20 million dollars from the sale of 1 million barrels of Brass. He has succeeded in blocking the price of his cargo of Brass at the level of $20 per barrel of 15 February. It is important to note that to obtain the result he had to make two opposing deals on the same financial market of Brent. That is, he has doubled the volume of paper business vis-à-vis the physical.

In our absolutely straightforward and simplified example, we have supposed that our man did nothing between 5 February and 15 March. In practice, however, he will have followed the fluctuations of the market day by day, entering it with purchase and sale deals of paper barrels, to take advantage of every opportunity to maximize the profits and reduce the losses.

For each physical transaction thousands of paper operations in the Brent market may be associated, to the point that this market becomes the most relevant and decisive to determine the mood of the market and set the price of crude. It must be said here that to cover the price risk, the strategy adopted by the various oil professionals is incredibly diversified and has changed over the years. Some companies, right from the start, have found in the risk hedging operations a fundamental way to maximize profits, to the point of making it an independent business with the creation of organizational structures detached from the physical trading of crude and petroleum products. They have, thus, created within their organizations a sort of financial group in competition with external financial institutions. Other companies have on the contrary tried to reduce the hedging activities to the bare vital ones, introducing very strict internal criteria for control and corporate governance.

Some companies that started out with the philosophy of the first group subsequently turned towards the second way of operating, often after suffering significant losses due to loss of control over the system and the excessive enthusiasm of certain traders (no-one can forget the historic banking houses that disappeared after the intemperance of some over-creative *rogue trader*).

Box 9.2   Second Example of Hedging

Now we will look at a second example, of how a company can implement strategies for hedging of its cargoes, cutting possible recourse to the Brent market down to the minimum. For simplicity, let us go back again to the example just elaborated and refer to the same characters.

We turn back to 15 March, when our commercial manager has concluded the operations regarding the cargo of Brass. Just at that moment he receives fresh advice from the terminal operator that on

29 March he must lift another cargo of 1 million barrels of Brass River. Since the market scenario is still the same, namely depressed and negative, he finds himself handling this second cargo, repeating exactly the process just concluded. So on the same day 15 March:

- He accepts the contractual commitment to sell a cargo of Brass River that he will lift on 29 March, at the price of Brent ruling on 29 March.
- He effectively sells (on the petroleum exchange) 1 million barrels equivalent of Brent at the price of $16 per barrel on the day of 15 March.

On 29 March the price of Brent will turn out to be $14 per barrel and he will complete, as in the previous case, the whole process by effectively selling and cashing in the proceeds from his purchaser of Brass (at $14 per barrel) and buying on the exchange (at $14 per barrel) the million barrels to close the new operation opened on 15 March with the purchase of Brent. Overall, this time too the balance of the situation is as follows:

	million dollars
1. Sale of 1 million barrels of Brent ($16/b)	+16
Hedging costs	
2. Purchase of 1 million barrels of Brent ($14/b)	−14
3. Sale of 1 million barrels of Brass River ($14/b)	+14
Overall result obtained	+16

This time too, the commercial manager has succeeded in blocking the selling price at the level of the day when he concluded the deal with the buyer, namely 15 March ($16 per barrel), thus avoiding the lower price on 29 March ($14 per barrel). In the context of the two physical sales, the paper market was used four times to carry out the hedging operations. We said earlier that depending on the commercial strategy of each company, these paper operations could multiply *ad infinitum* with daily actions on the oil exchange, such that the hedging operations for the two physical cargoes become almost a pretext.

In the case of a company that steers clear of financial speculation, is it possible to use the same technique of hedging of the two physical cargoes, reducing the number of the four operations executed in the previous example?

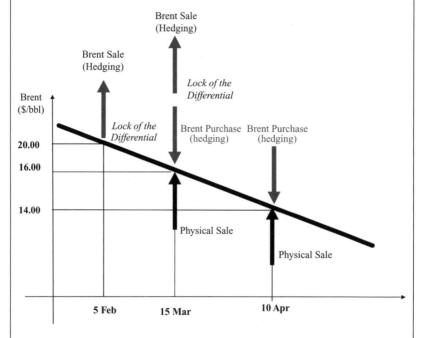

Figure 9.2 Example of integrated price-lock hedging

Let us summarize all the operations carried out by our man in the two cases:

	millions dollars
5 February	
1. Sale of 1 million barrels of Brent ($20/b)	+20
Hedging costs	
15 March	
2. Sale of 1 million barrels of Brass River ($16/b)	+16
Hedging costs	
3. Purchase of 1 million barrels of Brent ($16/b)	−16
4. Sale of 1 million barrels of Brent ($16/b)	+16
29 March	
5. Purchase of 1 million barrels of Brent ($14/b)	−14
6. Sale of 1 million barrels of Brass River ($14/b)	+14

We have already seen the economic results obtained by the totality of all these operations. Let us pause to examine only those actions executed on 15 March and in particular the fact that on the same day, and at the same price, the commercial manager has sold and bought the same item (1 million barrels of Brent paper), dealing with the same entity, the petroleum exchange. The first time he did this was to close his position regarding the first Brass cargo and the second time to open a new position for the second Brass cargo. From the economic viewpoint the process makes no sense. He could simply avoid making the two operations and still get the same result (saving the costs of the operations, which we have not discussed, but which exist).

In practice, however, the fact that the overall result does not change, even eliminating the two intermediate operations on the petroleum exchange, signifies that the hedging is anyway accomplished: but with what hedging mechanism?

The lucky coincidence that the date of the second sale is precisely that of the loading of the first cargo ensures that the second cargo acts as hedging for the first.

It is preferable not to complicate still further the example by going into real life where the complexity of the actual cases is obviously more detailed and requires somewhat more sophisticated techniques of application of the principles that have been illustrated. Let us limit ourselves to noting that it is possible to obtain an acceptable level of price risk reduction, and as such, a reasonable hedging effect, minimizing a recourse to the financial market by means of appropriate programming of:

- The dates of lifting from the various export terminals.
- The cargoes which are the property of a company or which have been purchased.
- The times in which to agree the sales' details with the purchaser.

Obviously, the more cargoes a company handles in a month, the greater are the possibilities of making this policy effective, that is, in which a cargo bought or sold protects the other cargoes in the month and is in turn protected by them. This technique is called portfolio hedging and it is certainly the one that implies the lowest level of recourse to the financial market, minimizing traders' temptation to speculate. To implement this hedging activity it is essential that a company is able to programme actively and dynamically the physical operations of loading at the various terminals, as well as the sales and purchases of outgoing crudes. A command panel that is effectively under control can generate enormous added value, often superior to what might be obtained through sophisticated trading techniques.

SPECULATIONS ON OPERATIONAL FLEXIBILITIES AT LOADING

At this point it is useful to give an example of how the paper market can allow and make possible certain forms of speculation by oil professionals. This explains why the loss of control of the price system by the producing countries and oil companies has not made many of them feel like orphans.

Box 9.3   Example of Synergies Between Operational Flexibilities and Hedging

We return again to a concrete example; on the famous starting day of the previous examples, 5 February, when our commercial manager is advised by the terminal operator of the date when he must lift his March cargo. Suppose that this time the loading date is 30 March (in the previous examples it was 15 March). When the manager goes into the market to try to sell the cargo he finds two purchase offers from his best client at these prices:

- the price of Brent on the loading day (30 March) exactly as it is; and
- the arithmetic mean of the Brent quotations in the month of loading, plus a premium of $1 per barrel.

He will have to decide which option to choose and then, eventually, reflect on his hedging strategy. In view of the uncertainty regarding the market in the following weeks (forecasts are always only forecasts), but considering a better price of $1 per barrel (which for a cargo of 1 million barrels means 1 million dollars), the commercial manager decides to accept the second offer and, thus, to sell the cargo not at the price of the loading date but at the monthly average of Brent quotations (see Figure 9.2).

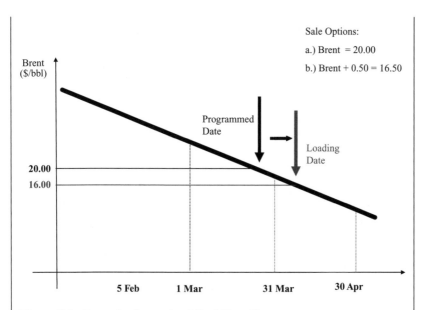

Figure 9.3   Example of operational flexibility effects

Let us see whether the decision taken was the best option. Suppose that once again the expectations for the Brent price are correct. Thus, on 30 March the crude price will be $18 per barrel and the monthly average for Brent until that day is $20 per barrel. Further, let us suppose that projecting the trend for Brent into the following month, it can be deduced that the April average will be around $16 per barrel. With these facts in hand, the purchaser decides to play his own cards to save $4 per barrel (meaning $4 million) on his deal. It is enough for him to telephone the captain of the ship navigating towards the terminal, to ask him to 'take it easy' and present himself at the berth only in the afternoon of 31 March. The consequence will be that the ship's loading process will inevitably end after midnight of 31 March, namely at the start of the month of April. Since the contract stated that the price would be calculated based on the monthly average of Brent in the 'month of loading', the purchaser will not pay $20 but $16 per barrel.

But this is not all. Suppose that the buyer of the cargo is a refining company of same oil company that owns the cargo. On the physical plane, the only effect will be a shift of income from one department to another within the same company. If the two entities are in different countries with different tax regimes there could be advantages or disadvantages deriving from a similar operation.

Now let us see what can happen if the physical operation in itself is associated with a vigilant activity regarding the futures (dynamic hedging). The seller as from 5 February knows that he has sold a cargo of Brass at the monthly average for Brent in March (first hypothesis). In this case his hedging plan will be different. Starting from the first day of March, he will sell every day on the petroleum exchange a quantity of Brent equalling 1/31 of 1 million barrels, thus striving for a selling price for his cargo that is equal to the monthly average ($20 per barrel). When on 30 March he sees the situation, he decides, together with his refining company, to 'shift' the cargo from 30 March to 1 April. That same day (30 March) he will close on the exchange the positions opened during the month and buy 1 million barrels of Brent at $18 per barrel (the day's price), succeeding in selling at the average price of the month ($20 per barrel) while having purchased at $18 per barrel, earning $2 million on the exchange. Moreover, the producing company will have to pay taxes on the cargo lifted based on the average price of the month of loading, namely on $16 and not on $20 per barrel. In addition, the sister refining company will have a cargo bought at $4 per barrel less, enhancing its refining margins.

Thus an operation is concluded with three net results:

- Earning $2 million on the exchange.
- A net reduction of the taxation basis in the country of production.
- Increasing the refining margin by $4 million.

Some examples have been given at the academic level so as to allow a glimpse of the complexities of the business that has developed with the birth of the paper market of Brent, Forward and Futures, whose interests have added to a business already exceptionally full of real risks. It is sufficient to reflect, just for a moment, on the size of the interests that hang over the management of the loading terminals in the various producing nations and how vital it is to ensure the transparency of the information regarding the process of assigning the dates for lifting the various cargoes.

In countries of unpredictable democracy and where the transparency of these processes is lacking, we observe a frenetic activity by trading companies that try to get their hands on crude supply contracts, although they do not have a refining system behind them or an adequate trading network. These firms try to acquire cargoes with especially favourable conditions (particular dates) that they can sell off to other more solid firms, sometimes earning a (huge) percentage of profit. Obviously the reality is much more complicated and those without adequate professional competences risk getting their fingers badly burned. The list of companies wiped out as a result of speculations that went awry is very long.

MARKET STRUCTURE: CONTANGO AND BACKWARDATION

In outlining the previous examples we made a series of simplified assumptions to illustrate the basic concepts involved. The realities of the market and industry practice today are obviously more complicated. Just to hint at some of the complex factors we refer to the so-called market structure. We have already seen how the 15 days Brent contract (even in its new forms) allows, every day, the purchase of a cargo planned for loading in the six months following the current one. The market transactions concerning these cargoes generate, each day, the forward quotations for the Brent price. Obviously, the forecast price for the future months fluctuates in line with market sentiments and the expectations of the professionals.

Two market situations emerge:

- **Contango**, where the Brent Dated price of today is lower than that of the subsequent months. This is the classic situation where a price increase is expected.
- **Backwardation**, where the Brent Dated price of today is higher than that of the subsequent months. In this situation pessimism prevails and the market expects a fall in prices.

Knowledge of the market structure allows and encourages many forms of speculation.

Box 9.4   Floating Storages

As an example, we may mention what happened in end-2008 and early-2009 – the speculation on whether crude cargoes were travelling or held floating 'on the water'.

During the month of December, the so-called market structure of Brent showed more or less this type of movement for the following months:

Month	Price, $ per barrel
December	43
January	48
February	50
March	52
April	54
May	56

This price structure offered the possibility for immense speculations. Anyone who had bought a cargo of crude in December for resale in December could have obtained a margin from the purchase and sale of commercial operations limited only to price fluctuations between the moments of purchase and sale, both values around the average price of $43 per barrel. If, however, he had succeeded in shifting the moment of sale to a following month, seeing the quotations of the following months, his margin would have become enormously greater. In the example, for a shift between December and May it was possible to arrive at $13 per barrel. For a cargo of 1 million barrels this would mean $13 million of additional margin. With the typical techniques of the futures markets it is possible to exchange (swap) the price of one month with that of another, earning the difference between the relative prices. Without entering into the technical details of the operation, we will just say that to consolidate the economic benefit, the transfer of ownership of the physical cargo – on which the speculation on the futures market is based – must pass from the seller (who is speculating) to his buyer in the future month selected as target for the price. It is easily appreciated that while the financial part of the operation on the futures market is relatively simple (it is only a play on financial transactions, stock exchange type), the physical part – maintaining ownership of the crude for months is not easy to achieve. In fact the cost of the ship and the associated risks (environmental and safety) must be taken into account. Since it is hard to find a buyer willing to accept these conditions of sale, the only way to achieve the objective is generally to sell to oneself, or to a related company. In practice, the tanker carrying the crude arrives normally at its destination. The crude is offloaded into the refinery storage tanks (rented by the seller), on behalf of the seller. The transfer of ownership will take place between the two sister companies at the most appropriate moment to maximize the margins of the operation. The net margin will be that guaranteed by the financial speculation less the logistic costs incurred. With a potential of $13 per barrel there is ample space to recover the costs.

PROCEDURES AT THE LOADING TERMINALS

From the examples we have just seen it is clear that the real value of a cargo of crude is not given only by the price of Brent on the day of loading, but by a series of factors that accompany the commercial negotiation and the eventual trading operations also involved, namely:

- the price differential agreed for that crude in that specific market situation;
- the hedging deals executed, to block the price at a level desired and possible;
- the eventual actions and operational flexibility taken at the moment of loading, with forward and backwards shifts of the loading date.

These are all actions that the birth of the Brent market has made possible and that can have a decisive effect on the final value of a cargo. In particular, the most glaring effects can be derived, as we saw in the previously elaborated, theoretical examples, from the combined play of operational flexibilities and oil futures. Many trading firms, whose main scope is speculative, are present in the business of the physical market for crude (buying and selling physical cargoes with all the risks and work entailed) instead of limiting themselves just to the game of speculation in the exchange, with the precise intention of taking advantage to make enormous profits inherent in combining these transactions. Obviously, for these actions to be possible it is necessary that rules exist at the various loading terminals which allow customers who present themselves with tank-ships to load crude to be able to utilize and exercise some flexibilities. It is furthermore evident that the oil company that also acts as terminal operator therefore has detailed information regarding production, storage and size of cargoes of the other partners and, with discretional powers over the flexibilities permitted, can obtain the maximum advantage in placing their own cargoes.

It is not unusual to observe within every joint venture bitter conflicts, often difficult to reconcile, when the so-called lifting procedures or off-take agreements come up for discussion: these are the rules that state how and when the various partners in a joint venture have the right and obligation to lift the cargoes they are entitled to. Normally the dispute regards certain fundamental matters. The first concerns the basic mechanism for the procedures, which may be of two types:

- The mechanistic method, which on a given day in the same month assigns the priority for lifting a cargo to the partner that on that day has accumulated the most barrels in the terminal storage facility.
- The nomination method, where the partners who in a certain month have the right to lift a cargo of crude inform the terminal operator of their desires regarding the loading date. The operator makes the final decision trying to satisfy the partners as far as possible.

Clearly the oil companies that act as operator (generally the majority partner in a joint venture) will try to impose the second solution, while the minority partners will try to defend themselves with the mechanical method. The dollars in play can amount to an enormous sum and can modify the degree of a partners' investment recovery.

Then there is another series of factors, apparently technical and operational, which nevertheless have a fundamental influence on the final value of a cargo. Just to give one example, depending on the logistics of the terminal, the standard size of the *nominal cargo size* that can be lifted at the terminal must be decided, that is, the minimum amount of crude that will be delivered to a ship arriving for loading. The major partners will try to impose the highest possible size for the nominal cargo, so as to increase the frequency of its own liftings and decrease those of the minority partners. In fact, a partner with a 40% share will accumulate more crude and quicker than one with only a 10% share. The greater the size of the nominal cargo, the longer is the waiting time for the minority partner to accumulate enough crude to allow him to lift a nominal cargo. For this reason, and wishing to establish the conditions of maximum operational flexibility for all the partners and potential customers at the Sullom Voe terminal, a nominal cargo of 500,000 barrels was agreed to for Brent, the smallest possible load that nonetheless has commercial value.

Another bone of contention between partners is the clause regarding the so-called *pooling of rights*, that is, the possibility of cooperation between two or more minority partners, to lift the barrels due to them and be considered as one sole partner having a participation equal to the sum of their respective shares. It might, thus, be possible for a new 'synthetic' partner to have a participation superior to that of the partner with the relative majority and/or function of operator, and thus be in a position to lift the collective cargoes with greater frequency (with significant advantages for a company's cash flow). Obviously, the game involving the distribution of the privileges and flexibilities has to be discussed. This is the reason for tenacious opposition and interminable discussions.

As mentioned previously, all this has a sharp impact on the value of a cargo of crude. It is one thing to try to sell a crude that is loaded at a terminal where all these flexibilities can be brought into play together, it is quite another to sell a crude to be loaded in a terminal where the operator allows the buyer no flexibilities whatsoever. The price can only reflect these differences, independently of the benchmark quotations on the day of loading. And often, for a standard cargo of a million barrels, it is a question of differences that can fluctuate around a sum of $10 million. For a partner in a joint venture, for the same investments made and costs incurred, the utilization of these operational flexibilities could seriously affect the time needed to recuperate such investments.

10

Problems of the Brent Forward Market

A separate chapter is dedicated to the distortions that have been created in the Brent 15 days market and the ways to remedy this. These are quite technical matters, but it is important to describe them, at least in general terms, to illustrate the dynamics that have permitted the creation of today's situation of almost total separation between the crude market and the price of crude. The fact that Brent became the worldwide reference benchmark had the consequence that every case of speculation on the Brent market translated automatically into a manipulation of the price of all the other crudes in the world. We can, therefore, understand the interest of Brent's controllers (and of some trading companies mainly operating in London circles) in wielding this tool and utilizing the flexibilities made possible, on the one hand, with the preoccupation of most of the producing countries that saw the price of their crudes in the hands of speculations perpetrated by a few operators. It is also for this reason that Saudi Arabia and Iran decided to uncouple the price of their crudes from Brent Dated, instead linking them directly to that of Brent IPE/ICE, where these problems cannot arise.

The most typical of these speculations was the so-called *Brent squeeze*. This was an operation for the temporary accumulation of paper and physical cargoes of Brent, normally carried out by a trading company, so as to remove them from the market, thus creating a shortage (undersupply of Brent) and panic, forcing players in the chain of 15 days Brent to purchase cargoes to meet their commitments and forcing many refiners to try to cover their requirements at any price. At the same time, the creator of the squeeze would buy numerous financial parcels of Brent on the futures market, artificially increasing demand expectations and consequently the price of Brent.

In the North Sea, given the short sea voyage (two to three days of navigation) and continuous availability of supply, many refiners buy their cargoes at the last moment. In the panic situation during the days of the squeeze, the price could rise abruptly (and did so) by as much as $2–5 per barrel. Having achieved his objective of raising the price, the trader who ran the operation came forward as the saviour of the motherland, selling the cargoes hitherto hidden and for enormous profits, even on the financial operations. Since all the crudes in the world are indexed to Brent Dated, but not restricted to only this reason, profits could be made on crudes from other geographical areas sold to third parties precisely during the days of the squeeze. We should not forget that Brent represents the benchmark for over 60% of worldwide crude: therefore, increasing the Brent price increases the price of all the crudes linked to it.

Obviously, the success of a squeeze operation depends on the ability to accumulate all the Brent cargoes in a minimum period (at least a week). With the reduction of Brent's production from 700,000 barrels per day (with about 40–45 cargoes per month, say 10 a week) to 200,000 barrels per day (with 12–13 cargoes per month, say 3–4 a week), the risk of a squeeze operation arose very frequently, making the value of Brent Dated completely unreliable. To block three or four loadings within one week became a feasible and frequently repeated operation for any trading company.

Box 10.1   Market Squeeze

Given here is a concrete example of a squeeze, now widely known, that was the proverbial straw that broke the camel's back. In 2000, a trading company (which we shall call Squeezer), with the help of other companies, was able to raise the price of Brent by about $2 per barrel for several days. Squeezer succeeded in making a market squeeze by buying early the September forward financial positions. At the same time, companies allied to Squeezer bought the entire physical market of Brent for the month of September, consisting of a few cargoes.

Against this background, at the close of the open financial positions, Squeezer requested the delivery of the cargoes bought in the Brent chain, cargoes that did not exist on the market (because they had been bought by its allies), and, therefore, obtained, as compensation, a significant monetary premium.

It was clear to everyone that the quotations of Brent Dated, under a speculative course, were no longer correlated to market conditions, but distorted upwards by actions orchestrated on the financial and physical markets. The graph in Figure 10.1 depicts what happened in the market during this episode.

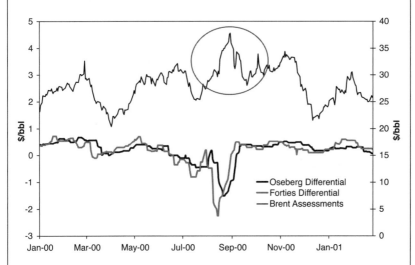

Figure 10.1 Distorted Brent Dated quotations

We can see clearly that:

- The North Sea market in September was obviously weak, as shown by the movement of the differentials for Forties and Oseberg, two crudes of higher quality than Brent, which became negative in that period.
- In contrast, the price of Brent Dated, parallel to the week of the squeeze and contrary to all the other similar crudes from the North Sea, registered a net and unjustified rise.

A US refiner, who right in that period had to buy some cargoes of Brent, contested the fraudulent behaviour of Squeezer and was awarded compensation by means of a lawsuit.

It is clear that an action of this type caused not only a rise of the price of Brent, but rather a distortion of the value of all the activities (financial and physical) linked to Brent itself. A manoeuvre like that made by Squeezer upset the entire market.

Something really had to be done to avoid such forms of speculation. An advocate for finding a solution to the problem was Platts, a McGraw-Hill owned specialized publisher of energy related periodicals that receives the support of industry professionals, analysts, traders, oil companies, university professors and government ministers.

Starting from July 2002, the historic contract for 15 days Brent was modified with the insertion of a series of new conditions and flexibilities of which the main ones are:

- the standard cargo increased from 500 to 600 thousand barrels;
- the delivery of the physical cargo could be accomplished by using two alternative crudes of similar quality, Forties and Oseberg; not only of Brent. The option to declare the type of crude was to be exercised two days before loading;
- cargo nominations were to be made 21 days before loading and not 15 days. In practice, spurned by the need to comply with the lifting rules at the terminals of the various crudes, the 15 day Brent became the 21 day Brent.

In this manner, a new benchmark was artificially created and expanded to comprise a basket of crudes, whose production permitted around 90–100 cargoes per month (say 20–25 a week). A squeeze would now require a financial and organizational feat that would be almost impossible for a trading company to instigate. The new market should now be named the 21 days BFO (Brent, Forties, Oseberg), but in industry parlance the old term, Brent contract, continued to be used. The BFO assessment envisages the daily value of Brent Dated as assuming the value of the most competitive crude among the crudes forming the basket; Brent, Oseberg and Forties.

The effects of this modification were clear from the start. The values of Brent Dated returned to normal, that is, below the assessment levels for Oseberg and Forties, and the squeeze problems disappeared.

The inclusion of Oseberg and Forties in the assessment also allowed for:

- a reduction in the degree of concentration of ownership of the various crudes, favouring greater transparency in the transactions;
- an expansion in the origin of the basket of crudes, which now included Norwegian crudes – governed by a tax regime separate and different from the UK tax system; and
- greater diversification of contract terms, since Brent cargoes respond to the GTCs (General Terms and Conditions) of Shell, cargoes of Oseberg respond to the GTCs of Statoil and those of Forties respond to the BP GTCs.

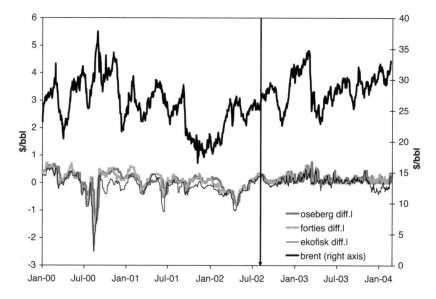

Figure 10.2   Movement of the benchmark before and after July 2002

As we can see in Figure 10.2, the benchmark, as from July 2002, began to follow the market trends of the other North Sea crudes, no longer presenting anomalous situations or unjustified price peaks.

We may, therefore, conclude that the passage to the BFO assessment was advantageous for the market and its players. The emergence of two new critical elements compelled a further adjustment to the BFO system at the beginning of 2007. These factors were:

- A new trend towards reduced North Sea crude production particularly in the crudes forming the benchmark (BFO).
- The coming on stream of a new field (Buzzard) inside the Forties pipeline system. This was a heavy sour crude that worsened the quality of Forties and hence the reference features of the BFO.

To compensate for the potential reduction in production and quality of the BFO, the international community, supported yet again by the forum of Platts, incorporated in the BFO basket the Norwegian crude Ekofisk. Ekofisk is a light crude with 37.5 degrees API and a sulphur content of 0.23%, thus transforming the BFO into *21 days BFOE*. The choice of Ekofisk, together with Forties and Oseberg, had the purpose of providing a safety valve should the value of Brent, normally the most competitive of the four, be manipulated for speculative purposes (upward squeeze).

Expectedly, due to the introduction of crude from the Buzzard field, Platts had to insert quality standards regarding Forties. Cargoes of Forties included in the BFOE assessment must have a minimum API of 37 degrees and a maximum sulphur content of 0.60%. For each percentage increase over the 0.6% threshold, a sulphur de-escalation factor applies in favour of the purchaser. If the sales contracts do not contain these two clauses, the sales of the cargoes are not taken into consideration for the purposes of estimating the BFOE.

The new assessment system was fine-tuned further to take account of the presence of the forward markets and the influence that they have in the final determination of the price of crude. Specifically, it was decided to refer, in the so-called market structure, to the situation of contango or backwardation.

Box 10.2   Assessment of Brent Dated (Platts' Methodology)

One must note that the assessment of Brent Dated has never changed name, either in its passage to BFO or when in 2007 it became the BFOE assessment. Purely to complete the information we shall try to summarize in a practical and concrete manner how the daily valuation of Brent Dated takes place.

Being the specialized source most adopted internationally, Platts' method will be utilized. In setting the daily valuation of the 21 day cash BFOE, Platts uses a system called Market on Close (MOC). MOC is none other than a system able to take account of all the values of the transactions effected within the 21 day BFOE contract at the end of normal trading hours in London at 16:30. Platts only considers arms-length (AL) sales, namely those negotiated openly in the assessment window. As already mentioned, the BFOE methodology envisages that the most competitive crude is the one that defines the value of the benchmark. In normal market conditions, Brent has always provided the benchmark. However, the introduction of Buzzard into the Forties stream has resulted in Brent often no longer being the most marginally competitive crude (see Figure 10.3). Thanks to this procedure for defining Brent Dated, the assessment always remains related to the fundamentals of the North Sea market, with the scope of reflecting the true relationship between demand and supply of these regional crudes.

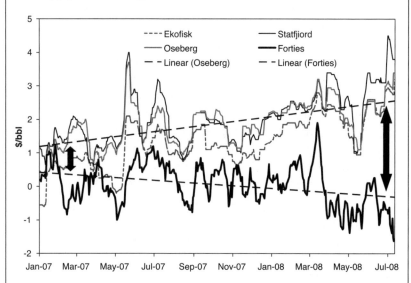

Figure 10.3   Relationship between demand and supply of regional crudes

The following example will show how Platts makes, today, the assessment of Brent Dated. Let us assume that on one particular day Platts has news of two different market transactions:

- a Brent cargo with window 16–18 July sold at Brent for August + $0.10 per barrel; and
- a Forties cargo with window 16–18 July sold at Brent Dated + $0.15 per barrel.

To reflect the market structure Platts must determine:

- The price of the Brent cargo on the basis of the value of August Brent Forward (whose assessment will be made based on the information available and the transparent movement of Brent ICE). If we assume that the value of Brent for August is $75.00 per barrel, then the price of the Brent cargo will be valued at $75.10 per barrel ($75.00 + $0.10).
- The price of the Forties cargo will emerge from a slightly more complex valuation. In fact, the value of Brent Dated will have to be estimated in the period 16–18 July, using a method that

refers to published data and is not subjective. Platts proceeds in the following way, weighing:
- the value of Brent for August, which we have assumed to be $75 per barrel; and
- from the CFD market (contracts for difference), Platts deduces the quotation of the value of the difference between Brent for August and the value of Brent in the week 15–19 July, namely the price paid by those operators who wish to modify a price agreement transferring the calculation of the average for Brent from one time reference to another (from the days 16–18 July to the average in August). Let us assume that in this case the market quotation for this type of exchange is 40.20 per barrel.
- The premium agreed between the parties is $0.10 per barrel.

Based on these elements, the price of the Forties cargo turns out to be $74.95 ($75.00 − $0.20 + $0.15).

It will, therefore, appear that on that day there were two transactions regarding crudes in the Brent Dated (BFOE) basket that gave rise to two values:

- $75.10 per barrel for the Brent cargo; and
- $74.95 per barrel for the Forties cargo.

Since the lower value is that of the Forties cargo, the value of $74.95 per barrel will be published as the value of Brent Dated BFOE on that day.

Obviously the same valuation process will have to be used for all the other days in the time span of 10–21 days used for the assessment.

The method of calculation for the assessment of Brent Dated has been modified over time, fundamentally to ensure the correct business procedure and to make life difficult for the cunning types who, to earn easy profits, could create enormous damage to the other operators by upsetting the balance of the markets. There is still the fact that it remains almost completely impossible to base price assessments on effective market transactions and to have to rely on the estimates, based on the behaviour of the futures market (ICE), made by the specialized sources. Consequently, the last word regarding what we call the oil price is now dictated by the financial markets, since the physical markets align with these without any possibility of reaction.

11
The European Refinery Crisis

In the previous chapters we saw that there is a financial oil market, where oil purchase and sale contracts are exchanged every day that do not involve the physical delivery of goods. There are purely paper markets, controlled essentially by the biggest banks in the world, which generate the number that we call the price of oil. Everyone assumes, even if it is not true, that the exchange of these paper contracts reflects in some way the dynamics between demand and supply of the commodity called oil. If you talk to a financial analyst he or she will confirm, believing it, that the movements in the price of Brent and the exchanges of the relative futures contracts exclusively and rigorously respect the fundamentals of the physical oil market. Since this high level of transactions has contributed, as a collateral effect, to keeping the price of oil at higher levels than that at which the physical market would have held it, almost all the players involved (e.g. producing countries and oil companies, governments etc.) have let the financiers play their game.

Only the collapse in prices in autumn 2008 reopened the discussion on the control of the price of oil. The rapid recovery of the prices in the spring of 2009, however, deferred the discussion to the next crisis. There is another collateral effect, unfortunately not made sufficiently clear, that the financial market is having on the oil industry and on the energy world in general. This is the potential progressive erosion of the margin of the refiner and hence of the future strategic position of the refinery industry.

The last refineries built in Europe and the USA appeared in the mid-seventies. From that time there have only been closures or upgrading operations of the existing plants. If you enquire about satisfying the oil consumption in the coming decades you will have to think about the construction of new technically more developed plants, but with the current low level of refining margins, these would not be remunerative investments. No private bodies could get involved in these activities, faced with negative results.

In the past decades refinery experienced crises of different natures and size. The most dramatic was at the start of the eighties when it had to deal with:

- the transformations of the energy market after the two oil shocks of 1973 and 1979; and
- the entry of the producing countries into the world refinery market.

The oil shocks have encouraged the growth and proliferation of nuclear power stations and the progressive transformation of the thermal power stations from fuel oil to gas, causing a collapse in the demand for fuel oil.

At the same time, the need and desire of many producing countries to expand their productive share and to recover increasing slices of oil revenues, led them to invest in the downstream, both by investing in refining and by acquiring distribution networks in the main consumer countries. Saudi Arabia, Kuwait, Venezuela and Libya are leading these trends.

The markets in the finished products are inundated with marginal low price products that will, however, become a new sort of benchmark for the whole international market.

The refiners find themselves in the situation of having to buy the raw materials at firmly fixed prices from the producing countries, and having to sell the finished products at the discounted prices imposed on the market by the marginal flows coming from the same countries.

The collapse of the refinery margins was inevitable. The sale of the refined products, at the new price levels, no longer allowed the raw materials and the refinery costs to be repaid.

Almost 50% of the refineries in the Atlantic Basin (USA and Europe) were unable to survive this transformation. This was a simple cycle for most of the refineries (those that were producing about 50% of the fuel oil) that were swept away by the market.

Only the refineries that either had already made investments to improve the production cycle or were able to build new conversion plants (those that transform fuel oil into gasoline and gasoil) survived. However, still more refineries survived, guaranteeing competition and productivity, in fact by improving the export facilities were able to expand the market hinterland and to make the structural export of gasoline to the US market (see Figures 11.1 and 11.2).

Following these dramatic transformations, the refining situation seemed to have stabilized in the second half of the nineties.

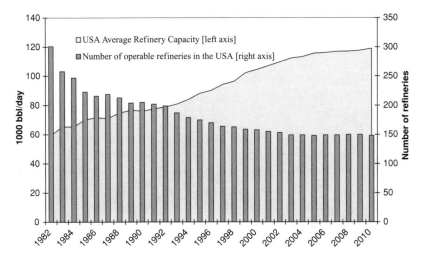

Figure 11.1   USA: number of refineries versus average refining capacity
Source: U.S. Energy Information Administration

Starting from 2000, the increase in the oil demand on the one hand, but above all the introduction of the new environmental specifications for vehicle fuels gave a new impetus to the refinery margins. The limited industrial capacity (by the majority of the operators) to produce refined products of high quality, as required by the new standards, led to

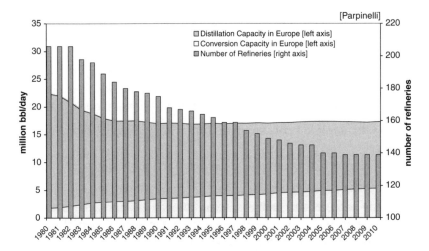

Figure 11.2   Europe: number of refineries versus distillation and conversion refining capacity

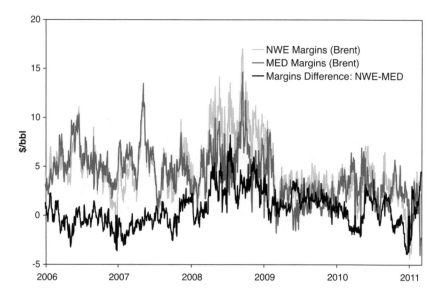

Figure 11.3   NWE and MED refinery margins: cracking plants

higher prices for the finished products also making the refinery margins leap ahead.

The price of the raw materials, which is something always available and potentially exceeding the demand, was in fact driven along by the products level.

For about six years the refiners recorded decidedly positive economic results. Slowly they began to talk about new investments and building new plants.

Then unexpectedly in 2009 came the new crisis (see Figure 11.3).

This new collapse of the margins was fairly difficult to understand and analyse. At first recourse was made to traditional models, citing:

- the reduction in oil consumption, following the global economic crisis; and
- the emergence of a consequent excess of refinery capacity, especially in Europe.

Having accepted this analysis, some companies approached the crisis by putting in place an exit strategy from the sector: partial or total closure or sale of the plants to concerns more integrated into the oil cycle (producing countries) capable of moving (or prepared to move) margins from one segment of the oil cycle to another, essentially for strategic, political or fiscal reasons.

Table 11.1   EUROPE: surplus/deficit in capacity, refining margins and demand

			EUROPE	
Year	Refining Capacity [kbbl/day]	Demand [kbbl/day]	Capacity Surplus/Deficit [kbbl/day]	Refining Margins [$/bbl]
2000	17,072	15,222	1,850	2.874
2001	17,150	15,393	1,757	1.459
2002	17,186	15,344	1,842	0.521
2003	17,278	15,468	1,810	3.152
2004	17,352	15,535	1,817	4.515
2005	17,370	15,673	1,697	6.783
2006	17,349	15,688	1,661	4.560
2007	17,305	15,454	1,851	4.797
2008	17,243	15,360	1,884	8.012
2009	17,069	14,498	2,572	3.583
2010	16,744	14,435	2,310	2.466

There is no doubt that the crisis in European refining, in a different way from the global crisis, is serious, profound and structural.

On the basis of the data available, in Europe against an oil demand of about 14.5 million barrels per day there is a refinery capacity of about 16.7 million barrels per day. There is therefore a nominal excess capacity of about 2 million barrels/day (see Table 11.1).

Obviously the difference between refining capacity and oil demand is not per se a measure of a potential negative imbalance or necessarily a cause of economic losses, for at least two reasons:

- Due to the historical trends in European refining, about 1 million barrels per day of products was exported to the US market.
- The net excess capacity (spare capacity) in Europe of about 1 million barrels per day means a lack of use of the existing plants of 6–7%, or a usage factor of 93–94% that, based on the historic data of this industrial sector, can be considered absolutely physiological.

In all the situations where it has been attempted to increase the usage factor above these values a high risk was often encountered. The large number of serious accidents occurring in American refineries is often due to the excessive increase in the usage factor.

Obviously, for a more effective analysis it is necessary to examine the distribution of the spare capacity according to the proprietary control, territorial distribution and import/export infrastructures with the network of the production system and the neighbouring markets.

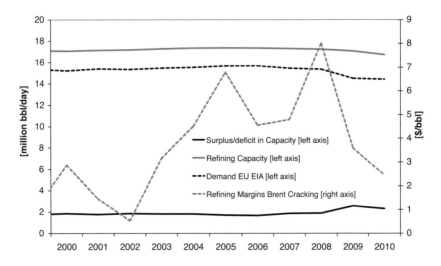

Figure 11.4 EUROPE: surplus/deficit in capacity, refining margins and demand
Sources: International Energy Agency and the author

Figure 11.4 clearly shows that the two curves of demand and refining capacity tend to follow one another.

There is a separation of the two curves in the years 2008–2010, when against a fall in demand of about 800 thousand barrels per day, there was a fall in refining capacity of about 500 barrels per day.

This represents a change in the usage factor of about 1.5%, due to a phase of economic crisis, which cannot on its own explain the collapse in the margins of the operators.

If the trend of the margins is observed, it can be seen that even at times of strongly positive values there is no surge in the usage factors of the capacity, just being limited to fluctuations of around 1%.

In the USA the situation is very different, even if it shows the constant lack of capacity against the level of internal demand (see Table 11.2).

The interesting element to be observed results from the combined analysis of the European and US refinery structures in Figure 11.5.

It is easy to see how in 2009 there was an effective fall in the overall oil demand of the Atlantic Basin of about 1 million barrels per day. This is a key value in the crucial moment of the crisis, which has already almost completely disappeared in 2010.

The persistence of heavily negative margins in 2010 cannot, therefore, be explained just or principally by the excess of spare refining capacity. There is clearly something new and complex not seen in the past, which

Table 11.2   USA: surplus/deficit in capacity, refining margins and demand

| | | | USA | |
| | Refining Capacity | Demand | Capacity Surplus/Deficit | Refining Margins |
Year	[kbbl/day]	[kbbl/day]	[kbbl/day]	[$/bbl]
2000	16,525	19,996	−3,471	2.006
2001	16,582	19,995	−3,413	1.315
2002	16,744	20,099	−3,355	0.743
2003	16,748	20,399	−3,651	2.946
2004	16,974	21,104	−4,130	3.648
2005	17,196	21,164	−3,968	9.760
2006	17,385	21,050	−3,665	7.320
2007	17,450	21,031	−3,581	9.300
2008	17,607	19,788	−2,181	5.628
2009	17,678	19,065	−1,387	3.862
2010	17,590	19,548	−1,958	3.890

Source: U.S. Energy Information Administration and International Energy Agency

requires a more sophisticated capacity of operation. In fact if a number of plants equal to the spare capacity (1 million barrels per day) were closed, the problem should be considered resolved.

This should produce with immediate effect a return to decidedly positive refining margins and the start of massive investment to meet

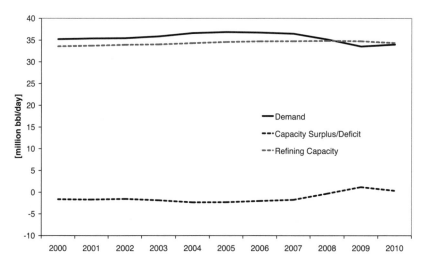

Figure 11.5   EUROPE and USA: surplus/deficit in capacity, refining capacity and demand

Sources: U.S. Energy Information Administration, International Energy Agency and the author

the technological challenges of the future, imposed by the qualitative changes in oil demand. Apart from the management of some social conflicts, if we were sure that this could be done, the problem could be solved quickly without asking for important economic sacrifices from the operators in the sector. Perhaps an in-depth analysis is worth while starting from considerations of good sense.

The market in finished products continued, even during the periods of collapsing margins, to be supplied without any form of interruption, meaning that we are not looking at a homogeneous cross-section in which all the operators find themselves in the same situation. The average calculated refining margins consider different situations especially if reference is made to the various geographical areas (e.g. Rotterdam, Mediterranean) and to the individual plants. Figure 11.6 shows how, against the changes taking place in the market of US gasoline, the refiners of Northern Europe have had a higher reaction capacity, producing suitable finished products and expanding their market share in the US market.

It is clear that these industrial and commercial policies have given these refiners economic advantages that are not visible in the values of the average standard refining margins published by the various sources.

Just to give an example, which is significant though not exclusive, a refiner that was able to export alkylate gasoline, especially in certain

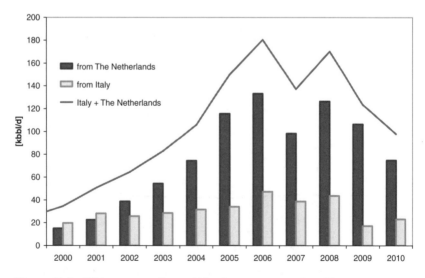

Figure 11.6 US import: gasoline and blending components from Europe

Source: U.S. Energy Information Administration

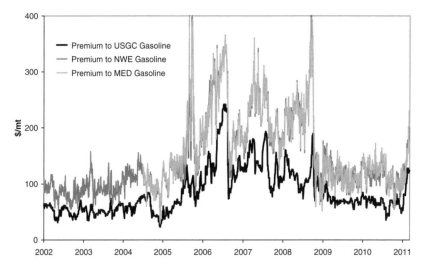

Figure 11.7 Alkylate premium to gasoline

periods of the year, should have been able to collect the extra margins (of at least $100 per tonne) above the price of gasoline (see Figure 11.7).

Only those refiners that continue to operate in this market segment have continued to obtain 'good' refining margins, despite the crisis factors. In particular, some differences can be explained in the performances of the refining markets in the two different areas of the European market (negative in the Mediterranean, supportable in Rotterdam). The different view of the market of the operators in the two areas has led to different investment policies in the last decade. In the Mediterranean, investment continued with the view of the eighties, namely sophistication of the plants to produce ever less fuel oil starting from heavy low quality crude oils. Above all they were operated to make refining a regional industry able to cover the local consumption. The potential hinterland of the market of the refineries was restricted.

There was only marginal investment in the transport infrastructures and export of finished products towards the more profitable markets. Some coastal refineries, with a high potential for export infrastructures, were closed or resized. In this context, Rotterdam has always been and remains a refinery base aimed at export. To get an idea of what has happened at Rotterdam, just take a tour of the oil port, where the refineries are an integral part of the port infrastructures, with thousands of tanks and loading wharfs for ships (and barges) of every size aimed for all the European, US and even Asian markets. These infrastructures give flexibility and, if managed with business sense, produce profits even in the difficult times of the market.

Returning to the previous argument, if in this framework the marginal operators who are no longer able to compete have to close the plants (1–2 million barrels per day), we will find ourselves in a situation that is very different from the nineties, when the capacity was decidedly greater than demand (almost double). In the context of the free market that exists between the two banks of the Atlantic Basin today, Europe finds itself in a similar situation to that of the USA, and should share the consequences of the structural deficit in the provision of finished products of the USA.

In fact, having balanced the European refining capacity at the level of the regional demand, to prevent the export of petrol to the USA it would be necessary either to establish duties (fairly improbable) or to be ready for an escalation in the prices to compete with the US consumers. In other words:

- The USA would no longer have the guarantee of the flows from 'safe and friendly' Europe.
- Europe would no longer be autonomous in the provision of finished products and could not count on a strategically reliable integrated area of support (the USA will have Europe, but Europe will not have another Europe for support).

So we are not able to face a dramatic collapse in the oil demand or a quantitative transformation such as to require draconian reductions in capacity. The problem is to adapt to the transformations in the quality of the demand, of acquisition of flexibility within the network of the demand of the Atlantic Basin and of a structural change in the management of the business in the face of the domain of finance in the control of the price of the raw materials.

We are, therefore, talking about a complex business in which the long term market view is important for making the appropriate investments as is the capacity to gather business opportunities day by day. In this regard we would like to add a basic consideration to the picture described up to now. For simplicity of explanation we would like to ask ourselves the following question: if a European refiner manages its plants in a perfect way, plans its activities taking account of all the transformations and evolutions of the international market and taking the opportunities that present themselves day by day, would it be able to obtain a refining margin that was so remunerative as to enable it to make investments for the total renovation of the plants: or, hopefully, to build a new refinery?

The reply is very simple and it's 'no', which means that, in the current situation, European refining is destined to remain an industry in slow structural decline and at risk of progressive obsolescence.

Here we arrive at one of the most virtuous contradictions and anomalies of the international oil market.

As we have already seen, the majority of the financial business is developed on the market of crude oil, namely the raw material. That of the finished product is only marginally involved.

For years now there has been a different dynamic in the evolution of the prices of these two markets. The price of crude is essentially determined by the trends of the financial exchanges in the stock market, on the basis of the market expectations of the bank analysts and operators, while that of the finished products continues to be fairly closely connected to the movement in supply and demand of the physical market.

The two trends are often divergent because of their nature and the instruments with which the players in the two markets operate.

The crude market alone appears to be sufficiently integrated both in the commercial dynamics and in the mechanisms that determine the price, while the market of the products is deeply fragmented according to product and geographical area.

The players in the physical market, the refiners, are used to operating according to the laws of the physical markets in which they operate and on which they place their products, seeking to identify the seasonal nature of the demand and scaling the supply accordingly.

They also try to acquire the crude with a time-scale that enables them to reduce their financial costs and the risk of the price changing between the purchase of the crude and the sale of the finished products. In the past these dynamics were determined by fixing the price of the crude and the finished products.

Today the price of the raw material is detached from this reality and depends on the expectations and dimensions of the business of the financial stock exchange.

The activity of the players in the virtual market is normally founded on expectations based on the statistical trends of certain variables considered to be fundamental by the financial analysts (spare capacity of OPEC, limitations of the supply, reduction in global reserves etc.) and on the technical analysis.

Having had several years experience of the repeated seasonal peaks of the price of US (and European) gasoline from April to August and that of diesel oil from November to February, with the consequent dragging of the price of crude, the financial analysts memorized the processes and changed their behaviour operating on the stock exchange so as to anticipate the seasonal phenomena. The massive purchases of crude (paper) take place at least one or two months before the expected phenomenon of the physical market.

This results in an increase in the price of crude in advance of the physical phenomenon and above the level that is only justified by the dynamics of the physical market of the products.

In putting this strategy in place, the financial operator is not taking any particular risk, in that he never finds himself in the situation of having to take possession of a single barrel of crude to be transformed into products. His job will be to buy one day and resell when the price has increased sufficiently. The provision in itself is just a pretext to justify taking the initial position on the market. The financial investor can 'escape' in a few minutes from the market in which he entered.

The impact of his action is, on the other hand, real and has an effect on the price of crude and the economics of the oil industry.

In our example, the refiner will have to buy the raw material at the price inflated in advance by the financial speculation but he will, however, have to sell the finished products at the prices (decidedly lower) imposed by the actual market. He will, therefore, find himself in the impossible situation of having to obtain satisfactory margins.

It seems to be a crazy mechanism without a way out that merits more in-depth analysis.

We have analysed the differences between the market dynamics in 2004 and those of 2010, two years in which the refining margins were different.

We have already said that the various oil products have a particular seasonal nature, which obliges the refiner to plan the procurement activities in a different way. In particular:

- Gasoline, for which the peak demand is between May and June (in preparation for the driving season). The necessary crude must be bought starting from March.
- Gasoil, for which the peak demand is in the winter months (being used for domestic heating). The necessary crude must be bought starting from the end of summer.

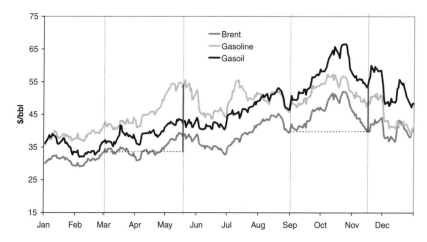

Figure 11.8 Brent and products prices 2004

Let us imagine evaluating the margin of a refiner operating in line with these criteria. Obviously, in order not to get into complex technical models, we will assume the extreme simplification that one unit of crude becomes one unit of finished product (gasoline or gasoil).

As our objective is to understand the dynamics and the mechanisms of reciprocal influence between raw material and product, the simplifications should not give us any problems. We have considered the fictitious margin of the refiner in 2004 (Figure 11.8) and 2010 (Figure 11.9), particularly significant years because they were less influenced by economic crises and political events in the major oil producing countries.

From the two graphs above, it seems quite clear that a theoretical refiner, who buys crude in March and sells gasoline in May, in 2004 earns $21.10 per barrel (gross of all costs, except that of the crude), that is about 63% of the cost of the raw material. Just six years later, in 2010, these earnings are reduced to $7.2 per barrel, that is (in the presence of crude prices that are more than double) a thin 9%.

As far as the crude bought at the start of September to sell gasoil in November is concerned, in 2004 our refiner earns $11.9 per barrel (about 29% of the cost of the raw material), while in 2010 this margin is $25.1 per barrel, that is about 33%.

Even if this data might seem comforting, we should remember that 2010 was a particularly cold year in Europe, so the demand for gasoil was significantly higher than expected.

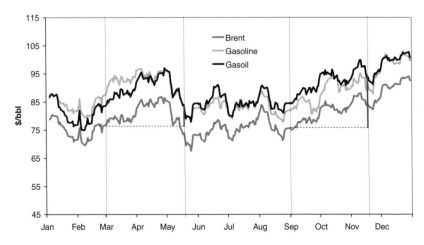

Figure 11.9   Brent and products prices 2010

It is also noted that both the products considered for 2004 are of an inferior quality than those used in 2010, to reflect the change of specification laid down for both. Gasoil in fact went from 0.2% sulphur content to 0.1 at the start of October 2007, and gasoline from 50 ppm of sulphur content to 10 ppm at the start of January 2009.

For this reason we should have expected the margins to increase and not substantially stay the same.

Now we will analyse the performance of Brent and products in our two reference years, assuming a price of 100 on 1 January each year. This operation enables us to analyse the variations for each commodity better, and to evaluate the reactivity in the peak demand periods.

In 2004 (see Figure 11.10), it is fairly clear that the prices of the products increase (with respect to their base value) at the moments of greater demand by the final consumers (mid-May for gasoline, towards November for gasoil).

At the same time it is noted that the price of crude increases following the greater demand on the part of the refiners, dragging the demand for the finished products.

In 2010 (see Figure 11.11), however, the relative increase with respect to the start of the year seems to be led by a much less marked seasonal variation, both for the products and for the crude.

We can still see increases in the prices of products at the moments of greater increase in demand, with the price of crude perfectly in line with

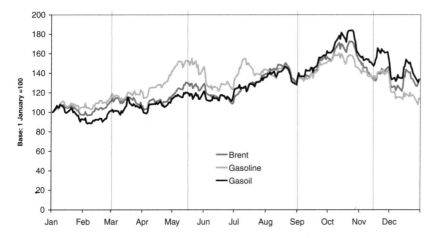

Figure 11.10   Brent and products prices 2004 (base: 1 January = 100)

that of the products – a sign of a new 'driver' in the crude market that slavishly follows or anticipates the movements in the product market.

Moreover, it seems that the prices of all three commodities are moving in a perfectly aligned way during the course of the year: this means that their percentage growth (with respect to the base value at the start of the year) is equivalent.

The phenomenon seems to be even more apparent if we look at the relationship between the prices of product and of crude.

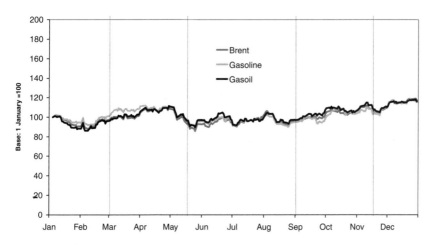

Figure 11.11   Brent and products prices 2010 (base: 1 January = 100)

Even though the refiner is not as interested in the ratio between crude and product as in the difference between the two (from the moment that his remuneration is marginal), it is important to study the percentage profitability of the principal products obtained.

This evaluation can help the refiner to plan the refining in a more coherent way, turning towards the products with greater profitability. By analysing the ratio we can understand whether it is better to favour a particular product at a certain time of the year, according to the logic of supply and demand.

It seems clear that in 2004 there were increases in profitability in the periods of the year of greater demand, while this was no longer happening in 2010. This consideration applies for both the products analysed. The ratio for gasoline, that was very volatile in 2004, seems to have levelled off six years later, and does not move substantially from values of around 1.1; moreover, the seasonal effect is much less evident.

This means that, while in 2004 the percentage profitability of gasoline varies considerably, and even reached 45% at the peak of the demand, in 2010 it stayed below 20% (see Figure 11.12).

Gasoil was subject to a similar fate (see Figure 11.13): while in 2004 a peak was noted in the ratio between November and December, reaching about 40% profitability at the peak of the demand, 2010 sees a much less marked seasonal variation, with profitability always less than 15%;

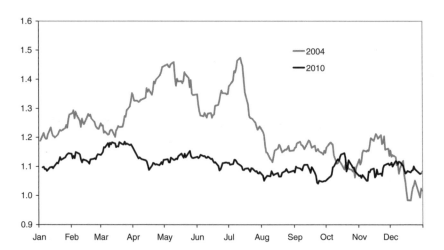

Figure 11.12   Gasoline/Brent prices ratio

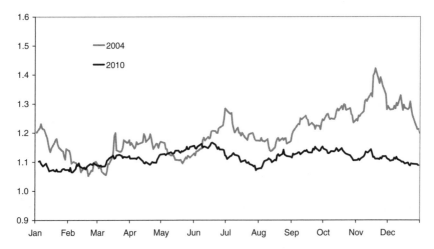

Figure 11.13   Gas oil/Brent prices ratio

even in December, at a time of greater tension in the physical market, the profitability was only 10%.

Having seen the dynamics of the two markets of crude and of finished products, it is clear that it was the crude market (financial and extremely flexible) that adapted itself to that of the products, anticipating any minimal variation and sweeping away the traditional possibility of the refiner buying in advance in view of the seasonal nature of the demand for the products. This led to the erosion in the earnings on products even in the period of greater demand.

In practice, the new sophistication of the financial markets consequently led to the substantial transfer of most of the refining margin from the refiner to the financial investor. We are facing a situation in which the market is no longer able to generate reactions to correct the mechanisms of exaggerated speculation.

It would be logical to expect, under normal conditions, that a reduction in the margins would correspond to a reduction in the work on crude in the refineries and hence a reduction in the supply of finished products with a consequent increase in the price of the products and finally a rebalancing of the margins.

In our case, the financial speculation has such a capacity to intervene (due to its size and timing) as to neutralize these mechanisms of the physiological reaction of the market. The increase in the finished products that should allow the improvement of the margins is separate from the immediate rise in the prices of crude (paper), condemning the refiner to a structural loss. It is the perverse effect of Uranus who ate his children.

What do you do in this absurd situation?

It would be hoped that the problems raised by this situation might become the subject of the political and energy policy of the various industrialized countries, but the individual operator cannot avoid looking for his or her own survival strategy. In a world dominated by the financial mechanisms, the solution has to be sought in that very context with the use of certain instruments offered by the world of finance.

It has created, as well as the crude market, a world of virtual refining, in which it is possible at any time to buy paper barrels, to process them in a virtual refinery and to sell the finished products obtained, achieving a refining margin. This margin is called the 'crack spread'.

A refiner who operates in the real world of the oil industry can associate his daily activity with certain operations in the virtual world of financial refining, trying to combine the relative margins of the two parallel activities. Obviously the technicalities of the market are complex and varied. What is worthwhile emphasizing is how the virtual refining process, if suitably managed, enables higher margins to be achieved than real ones (see Figure 11.14).

Figures 11.15 and 11.16 show how in the last two years the difference between crack spread and real refining margin registered a value of $5–15 per barrel.

Therefore, a refiner who knows how to combine his or her activity in the real market with the parallel and systematic activity on the financial market is in a position to achieve overall results that enable the margins for the real activities to be improved in net terms. It is not the solution to the problem, but a way of managing it.

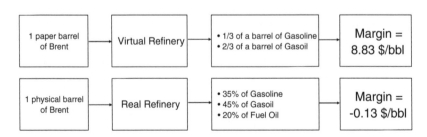

Figure 11.14 Comparison between a financial refinery and a real refinery (MED, January 2011)

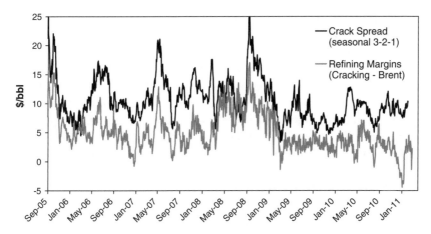

Figure 11.15   NWE: refinery margins (cracking plant) versus crack spread (seasonal 3–2–1)

We are, therefore, looking at an industrial problem that has complex strategic implications, such as, for example:

- Historical interdependence between American and European refining.
- Level of technological sophistication of the existing plants.
- Crisis and limitation of the import/export logistics.
- Control of the financial oil markets.

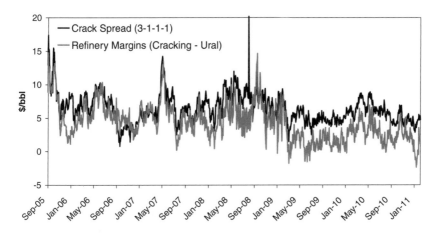

Figure 11.16   MED: refinery margins (cracking plant) versus crack spread

The problem lies in the future, in at least the next two decades, in which we will still have a fundamental need of fuels for transport (gasoline, gasoil, jet fuel).

There will need to be an industrial plan of European and US investment that enables security of supply to be achieved within this time horizon. This will mean adopting decisions that are not too dissimilar from those taken in face of the crisis in the automobile sector, hopefully before the crisis blows up with very devastating impacts.

The worry is that nothing will be done, in that the size of the problem still does not seem to be appreciated.

It is the author's belief that, if similar considerations could be extended to other sectors of the financial markets (e.g. food), the reasons for the difficulties and the enormous resistance that exist for any plan to reform these markets and the international stock exchanges would be clearer.

Box 11.1   Trends in Agricultural Products and Oil Prices

The link between agricultural products and oil prices can be taken into consideration to understand some of the aspects of the current North Africa crisis.

Let's start by looking at some data, in Figure 11.17, on the evolution of the demand and the prices of oil and food products in the last 10 years.

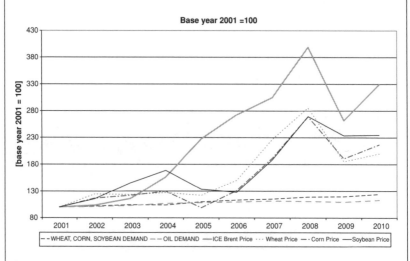

Figure 11.17   Agricultural and oil demand and prices

From 2001 to 2010, the demand for oil, like that for the food products, increased by 20–25%. In the same period the prices of oil increased by about 350% and those for food products by up to 280%. We are looking at a price dynamic that is running on average 10 times above the level of demand, despite being in the presence of a fairly balanced supply. The analysis of the data shows how the increase in the price of food products has been relatively lower than that of oil. The increase in the prices of food products becomes significant, among other things, only starting from 2006, while that of oil is already evident from 2003. This means that, for the various producing countries, the oil revenues have been higher than the costs sustained for importing food products.

It would have been logical to expect that this difference between oil revenues and costs of food products would transform itself into an increase in the per capita income of the populations of the countries concerned. On the contrary, if we look at the published data in Figure 11.18, we can see that (with the exception of Libya) the level of the per capita income during the same period only increased by 10–30%, in line with the increase in the actual demand for the food products consumed. That is, the increase in income was not even allowed, given the level of increase in the prices, to continue to develop as in the past.

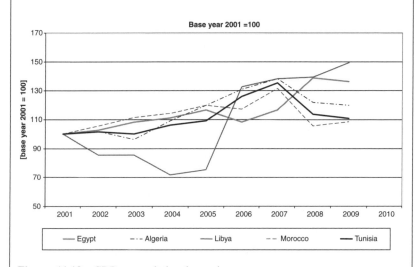

Figure 11.18 GDP per capital and open interest

So, two simple questions arise:

• How have the rising oil revenues been used in the various countries in the past 10 years?
• Given the development of the effective demand for the various goods, against a substantial stability in the supply (in some cases even a supply surplus), what causes these enormous increases in the prices of raw materials (oil and basic food products)?

The answer to the first question is in all the papers and refers to the scandal of the distribution of wealth in the various oil countries where minority groups of the population, which gravitate around the families of the various leaders, are able to accumulate enormous fortunes, which are invested and spent in the most luxurious areas of the major metropolises of the world. It would suffice to draw up the lists of the property assets in London, Paris and New York to get the picture. Like the flow into these countries of the most expensive sports and luxury cars. It is astonishing to discover that in some cities of the Middle East there are more Rolls-Royces than in the whole of Europe.

The most alarming aspect of the gap between oil revenues and pro capita income is the impoverishment of the middle classes. In the past three to four years it turns out that even fairly high level state officials or state company employees are no longer in a position to guarantee an acceptable standard of living. A real explosive cocktail waiting for a detonator.

To answer the second question it is necessary to examine some more data.

Figure 11.19 shows that starting from the mid 2000s an activity was triggered on the parallel futures markets for oil and food products. The exchanges of 'paper' contracts of grain are multiplied by more than seven or eight times with increases of 400%, indicating a new hunting ground for international finance. The food market became another refuge for the monetary mass of the international banks. It can also be seen how, once the moment of crisis of 2008–2009 had passed, the activity in the futures on these raw materials restarted with more strength than before.

The result of these activities on the virtual markets is the aggravated increase in the prices of these goods on the physical markets and,

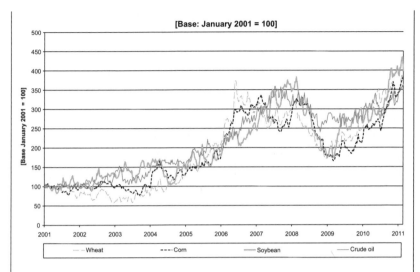

Figure 11.19 Agricultural and oil futures open interest on NYMEX

hence, an aggravation of the social problems of the poor part of the population. Once again we are facing a case of the potential disastrous effects that the financial market can have on the physical economy and the real word. The financial speculation has penetrated deep into the mechanisms of the production/physical systems and is tending to deform its operations beyond the normal physiology of the markets.

A realignment of the virtual markets with the real ones could have a dramatic result for the banks in the short term, but perhaps this process will be unavoidable at some point.

In the meantime, in the oil sector, this climate of expectation brings concrete and immediate benefits to the producers of the raw material (producing countries and oil companies), but, as we have seen, is also having dramatic effects for the refinery industry.

The phenomenon is becoming dramatic in the western areas of consumption, where the economy is strongly dominated by the financial markets. It is almost paradoxical to see that the only countries that are investing in the refining sector are China and India, where the state intervention in the management of the real economy is still determinant. They are the countries that are looking to the future, beyond the contingent crises and the uncertainties of today's market.

In the west the false conviction often prevails that the liquidity of the financial markets corresponds to an excess of capacity of the production systems. At this rate, if nothing is done, together with the tomatoes coming from China we will begin to depend on the supply of oil products from China and India. At that point, we will have to be ready to pay very high prices, given the competition which we will have to face on a global level.

Perhaps it would be more reasonable and advantageous, economically and socially, to dig deep into our pocket and invest massively in the refinery technologies and plants. This is a much more important priority than the construction of new nuclear power plants.

12

Conclusions: We are
Ourselves OPEC

In the recent past, following a big rise in oil prices, a debate took place regarding two highly sensitive themes: the clash of civilizations and the reactivation of a programme for the construction of nuclear power stations. These are two distinct themes, apparently unrelated to each other. Yet it is singular that the discussion began and expanded in coincidence with the materialization of the said initial event, the rise in oil prices. Having reviewed these themes, no pretences are being made that there are additional or resolute facts to add to those already circulated by the world's press. It is, however, important to relate the themes we have covered here to the basic model of reasoning which we have developed in our discourse. It is certainly positive that a discussion regarding nuclear energy goes ahead in a spirit that is critical, constructive and supported by hard facts. By moving away from emotional responses to the oil price alarm, we can move forward and adopt an approach based on economic, technological, environmental and strategic terms.

In this sense we should clearly envision what we have already elaborated on in the preceding analyses. Today, the fundamental question of the price of oil is linked to a lack of refining capacity and adequate transformation technologies for producing clean transport fuels (gasoline, gasoil, jet fuel). This problem essentially concerns the industrialized countries who have created growing and unchallengeable environmental legislations, but who have not provided sufficient investment incentives for the development of technologies and plants (for production of cleaner products) in the refining sector. Today the production of electricity has no direct impact on the price of oil: the fuels for power stations are residual products available in excess. The choice of nuclear power for a country should be of an overall strategic nature: that of being in one of the advanced technology sectors where scientific research can be a fundamental and decisive factor for advancement in other sectors. This was actually what many hoped would happen in Italy, even after the 1987 referendum: to at least keep afloat the existing plants to allow for the conservation of know-how and maintain participation in worldwide scientific research. This brings to mind what happened in Europe when the rich and powerful Italian marine republics refused to finance the challenge proposed by Christopher Columbus. They were not stimulated to expand their technological capacities to build ships able to face the waves of the Atlantic. Countries like Holland and Portugal, far behind Italy at the time, accepted the challenges of the ocean and benefited from remarkable developments. Perhaps they were helped by the fact that their shores were washed by seas beyond the Columns of Hercules; there was, thus, no debate on whether to pass through them. Italy was destined to an inexorable decline and, locked within the increasingly limited Mediterranean market and restricted by the cultural climate of the counter-reform and the Council of Trent, was cut off from all the scientific processes and technological research of those centuries.

One positive outcome of a debate over nuclear power would be if it once again causes us to face up to the challenges of the technological frontier. In this case, we will also have to get involved in the challenge of research on automotive fuels that will enable us to overcome the crisis of today (unfortunately the solution is not bio-fuels; too easy an answer). Countries that for over 40 years have been the giants of the world refining industry cannot sidestep this challenge, of which full awareness seems not to exist to date.

The environmental challenge has been, till now, a sort of problem for the elites of the industrialized countries. Fuel laws have become effective and strict in western countries, leaving emerging countries like China and India, where the air in the cities has become unbreathable, out of the picture. If we assume that in the space of a decade these new consuming countries will move in the same direction as western countries, the system will reach the point of collapse: there will not be sufficient clean fuels for everyone. The refining systems which exist today will be unable to produce clean fuels, starting from the crude oils available. An economic commitment and a project for technological research and industrial investments of enormous proportions will be necessary, for which today's downstream industry is not at all prepared nor motivated. Is it conceivable to think of dedicating a part of the huge amounts of tax paid on petroleum products to these projects?

Too often the debate over oil is concentrated on the size and duration of the reserves. Certainly this aspect of the problem exists and has to be considered, even if it is not the key issue that concerns the citizens and inhabitants of planet Earth. And, above all, when it is invoked to justify an increase in crude price, it is really out of place. The fuels we need can be obtained using varying technologies starting from the most disparate raw materials: from crude oil to natural gas, to coal, even up to bio-components. There is ample availability of these. The problems in production of clean, environmentally compatible fuels are related to technology and costs. Let us just think about the development of GTL (gas to liquid) technology, namely the production of extremely clean, high-quality liquids, starting from gas. Not only do we know that there is still enormous availability of natural gas, but that coal can also be gasified, and from this gas clean liquids can be produced. There is no need to remember that these are ancient technologies (to be re-studied and improved) used, for example, in South Africa during the embargo years. Implementation of these technologies will depend on investments made in research, on overall production costs, but also on the flexibilities that the automobile industry will provide in the future. Engines designed to function with liquids structured in a different way from the traditional gasoline can make the use of these new products easier.

It is clear that, facing (and on the eve of) far-reaching changes that can affect the world oil scenario, asking the refiners, who are the most conservative and traditional members of the oil industry (at times referred to as 'petroleum peasants'), to expose themselves today to the risk of heavy but ultimately excessively risky investments, would be a pure illusion. The tensions we are facing up to tell us that the break-even point for the use of different raw materials is now very close. If, when analysing the future scenarios, the outcome of the environmental problem in the Far East were taken into serious consideration, the decisions that would have to be taken would appear more linear and less exempt from risk. Investments in downstream petroleum technologies should be much greater and less tentative than they have been in the last three decades. Within 10 years we could easily discover that someone else has taken the situation seriously and is guiding the new technological processes and the production of new fuels. Somewhat similar to what happened to the Italian marine republics.

The obsession, almost exclusively focused on company share values as examined by financial analysts and presented to shareholders every quarter or half-year after, increasingly risks locking companies into policies that are targeting only short-term results. Without intervention from national or supra-national institutions, this picture will not change and there will be no move towards a solution on the basis of free market forces.

Discussion of these themes should have progressed in concrete and scientific terms in the last 10 years, but unfortunately there have been frequent attempts to sidestep the problem, taking refuge in pointless exchanges. The most glaring example was the debate on the clash of civilizations, or on religion, which produced a sort of metaphysical sublimation of the attempt to defend the status quo. The author has several Nigerian friends with important jobs in the State administration, with whom he has had the occasion to discuss the so-called religious conflicts that have characterized Nigeria's recent history. They explained, in detail, how the tensions and conflicts were manipulated and amplified to enable the heads of the various ethnic and social groups to demonstrate their political weight in the mediations to develop in the centres of power of the capital. No one had ever raised the problem of contesting the religious faith of other persons. And one finds an immediate example of that when, travelling between villages, Christian churches and Mosques of all types are seen, well distributed throughout the land. However, from time to time, one cannot avoid seeing manifestations of violence. The key problem is in the division of the oil revenues between the poor regions (with a Christian majority) where the oil is produced, and the richer regions (with an Islamic majority) where most of the revenue arrives. With the increase or decrease in the flow of petrodollars, everyone feels entitled to renegotiate previous agreements with all the tools at their disposal, including using an ideology of religious differences and the ensuing violent encounters. The author believes there is not much difference between what happens in this country as characterized by the historic co-existence between peoples of different religious creeds and what is happening around the globe. At the cusp of a crucial crisis between availability of energy resources and prospects of increased demand, the world is rediscovering that hydrocarbon reserves are distributed across the globe in a very heterogeneous way and are concentrated in certain specific regions of our planet, where Islam is prevalent.

During the 1990s, the growth of crude production in the North Sea and domestic production in the US allowed for the creation of a futures market. The internal mechanisms of the financial markets have created a powerfully expansive trading game, where as a founding principle the sensation of an unlimited supply, readily available everywhere, has permitted the removal of the physical aspect of the market, namely the authentic aspect. The basic principles of management of the oil companies and the refining organizations have been overturned. The operational programming of the production cycle has become a secondary element vis-à-vis the achievement of the overall result. In some organizations, the risk management department, which handles operations in the futures market, has become an autonomous business hub, often the fulcrum of all the trading activities. All this has been strongly supported by the tax legislation of some European and US states, where trading activities have enjoyed important fiscal benefits.

Financial instruments have become, as it were, a new religious faith, whose sole priests are very young traders, fanatics and millionaires, experts in market techniques. This explains the clamorous events in which individual traders have triggered the fall or bankruptcy of venerable world financial institutions (see the much publicized case of the Société Générale). This is a market that is becoming ever more self-serving and controlled by the managers of world finance. The movements of crude prices have proved to be linked more to the horizontal operations of finance (shifts of funds from one asset to another) rather than to the internal dynamics of the oil market, such as those of demand and supply. Quiet reflection would be necessary, well away from the fever of the financial religion which has dominated these last few years. Only in the last decade, the prevalence of the unflinching trust in finance has brought us down a path that has resulted in the further deterioration of the situation and taken us further away from a possible solution.

It is difficult to ask the priests of these new religions, highly technological but also very fanatical, to formulate a logical, historical and political approach to the problems of energy and oil. It is easier to continue speaking about a west surrounded and attacked by another religious universe that is also in control of the availability of crude. This allows the world to postpone, still further, any concerted quest for solutions to the problems at hand, instead permitting the financial arena to grab further profits.

The author believes that a major part of the debate over the clash of civilizations takes place at the abstract level, which does not get to the root of the problems. Right from the start, the confrontation between Islam and Christianity has been affected by the control of the Mediterranean economy. Today, it has to take account of the control of the energy market and distribution of the oil revenues. It may seem trite to say this, but a true process of stabilization of peace can only start from a reconsideration of the technology of private transport and the replacement of the traditional service stations. We may conclude our narrative by recalling a fable of Aesop, that of the horse, the boar and the man. The horse, accustomed to drinking at a fountain of fresh crystalline water, one day sees a boar dirtying the spring water. To resolve the problem, the horse decides to ask for the help of a hunter, who riding the horse follows and captures the boar. With the task completed, the man discovers the usefulness of the horse and decides to put a rope round his neck so that he cannot escape. If we change the names of the actors, putting the oil companies in place of the horse, the turbulence of the market in place of the boar and the futures markets in place of the man, we have a snapshot of what happened in the last two decades. All the actors in the productive cycle of oil have delegated the management of their company's risk to the financial fund managers, who at the end have become the true masters of the business, dictating rules, limits and perfecting the strategies. The lesson that the financial crisis has given us should make us understand that the links between finance and oil are very tight and full of risks for the future.

The events that during the first few months of 2011 upset the political scenarios of North Africa and the energy markets of the Mediterranean require an examination that goes beyond the possible future changes in the control of power in the various countries.

We are therefore facing a crisis scenario in which it seems clear that the power of finance, which in fact means that of no more than a dozen banks in the world, is today boundless and devoid of any political control.

There is nothing new in saying that the power of finance and the banks is boundless, but it is new to see the new dimension of the phenomenon on a global level, which can intervene in the political and social equilibriums of entire regions in the world and of the development of strategic sectors of the global economy. I remember learning from the books at high school that the wars of the 16th century were decided in Antwerp, the financial capital at the time. In an era when armies were not made up by national troops but by mercenaries, obtaining the financing from the banks was fundamental to equipping soldiers and having the chance of winning. Indeed in order to keep Antwerp under control, Charles V, the emperor of Spain and the Holy Roman Empire, did not live in Madrid but in Brussels. There was, therefore, a form of control of political power over international finance.

Today seeing this immense power devoid of control and causing apparently devastating effects, leads us to ask how all this could be possible. It is possible to fantasize about scenarios of the type described by Orwell in 1984, with a Big Brother intent on using its financial power to achieve its objectives, but we know that the complexity of the world does not permit these simplifications. So we need to look at two possible alternatives. One is the existence of a neo-liberal and monetarist economic target at a global level agreed by the majority of the governments of the economically strongest countries, which, however, is starting to break up and to cause unexpected and unwanted collateral effects. The other is that there is no longer political leadership at a global level able to call upon a capacity for governing these power centres.

The developments after the financial crisis of 2008/2009 incline more to the second. The banks were saved by the governments without any attempt to at least change the rules of the financial markets. When Obama tried to open the Wall Street dossier he had to shut it again immediately. There are no new Roosevelts, Churchills or De Gaulles around.

If we put together the messages that are coming from Japan with the Fukushima disaster and from Libya with the shutdown in the production of crude almost all of light quality (ideal for the production of high-quality petrol), we see once again how the control of the market in hydrocarbons continues to have a strategic bearing for all the industrialized countries. In the next few months we will already be seeing the effects of these events at the petrol pumps. So, despite the evidence of this strategic impact of oil (as indeed that of food products) this raw material will still be allowed to be subject to the most devastating financial speculation.

Karl Marx describes a world in which the owner of a factory and his worker represent the two class enemies par excellence. Today they are both like straws in the wind dragged along by a devastating current. Perhaps we can continue to talk of the world with models that worked up to a few years ago, but that no longer allow us to deal with events that are taking place at a pace unknown before in the history of humanity. In this framework politics seems too often to be inadequate, bewildered and incapable of understanding and guiding the economic and social processes. And we will continue to see the price of fuel increasing at the service station, at least so long as we continue to produce it in our refineries.

Every time we stop at a service station to fill up the car we should be aware of the complex universe that is inside every drop of liquid that the pump delivers. Above all, we should realize how precarious the equilibrium is, which allows us, despite complaints about the prices we have to pay, to receive a fuel that is sufficiently clean, readily available everywhere, without having to queue or worry about the next fill-up.

This is not something to be taken for granted and this applies to anyone who travels around the world. In too many countries this service is not guaranteed and perhaps it will be even less so in the future, with the resulting tensions that we can easily imagine. And these tensions foster powerful financial speculations.

All this can and must change, but it will require a radical cultural transformation on the part of both consumers and producers. We might say that it will take generations for this to happen, but we do not have this time. Solutions are needed more quickly than our habits and laziness allow. Someone in the past decade has tried to coerce the global equilibrium so as to guarantee the status quo of our way of life and thinking, but with disastrous results.

The only way now is to force us to understand and find the right solutions. We cannot now put our faith in any OPEC, whether Christian or Muslim. Now, we are OPEC.

Bibliography

Annual report 2009 (2009) Unione Petrolifera.

Augieri, Giuseppe (2002) *Cambiare per sopravvivere: la questione energetica in Italia*, Rubbettino Editore Srl.

Banks, Ferdinand E. (2000) *Energy Economics: A Modern Introduction*, Kluwer Academic Publishers.

Castagna, Luigi (2008) *Il pianeta in riserva. Analisi e prospettive della prossima crisi energetica*, Edizioni Pendragon.

Clô, Alberto (2002) *Economia e politica del petrolio*, Hoepli.

Clô, Alberto (2008) *Il rebus energetico*. Tra politica, economia e ambiente, Il Mulino.

Clô, Alberto (1990) *Interdipendenza e instabilità nell' oligopolio petrolifero*. Lezioni di economia industriale, CUSL.

Davis, Jerome D. (2006) *The Changing World of Oil: An Analysis of Corporate Change and Adaptation*, Ashgate Publishing Limited.

Eden, Richard John (1981) *Energy Economics: Growth, Resources, and Policies*, Cambridge University Press.

Energy Policies of IEA Countries – the United States of America 2007 Review (2007) International Energy Agency.

Energy Policies of IEA Countries – Italy 1999 review (1999) International Energy Agency.

Fattouh, Bassam (2007) The drivers of oil prices, Oxford Institute for Energy Studies.

Gary, James H. and Handwerk, Glenn E. (2001) *Petroleum Refining: Technology and Economics*, Marcel Dekker.

Gary, James H., Handwerk, Glenn E. and Kaiser, Mark J. (2007) *Petroleum Refining: Technology and Economics*, CRC Press.

Horsnell, P., Brindle, A. and Greaves, W. (1995) The Hedging Efficiency of Crude Oil Markets, Oxford Institute for Energy Studies.

Jovinelly, Joann (2007) *Oil: The Economics of Fuel*, Rosen Publishing Group.

Krugman, Paul R. (2002) *International Economics: Theory and Policy*, Addison Wesley.

Legge, Sarah (1997) A Comparison of the US and European Auto/Oil Programmes, Oxford Institute for Energy Studies.

Lerche, Ian and Noeth, Sheila (2004) *Economics of Petroleum Production: Value and Worth*, Multi-Science Publishing Co.

Mabro, Robert (1992) OPEC and the Price of Oil, Oxford Institute for Energy Studies.

Mabro, Robert (1998) The Oil Price Crisis of 1998, Oxford Institute for Energy Studies.

Mabro, Robert (2005) The International Oil Price Regime: Origins, Rationale and Assessment, *The Journal of Energy Literature*, XI(1).

Mabro, Robert (2006) *Oil in the 21st Century: Issues, Challenges and Opportunities*, Oxford University Press.

Matteo, Falcione (2004) I contratti del mercato del gas naturale, Eliconie Editrice (collana AIEE).

Maugeri, L. (2001) Petrolio, Sperling & Kupfer.

Maugeri, L. (2006) *L'era del petrolio. Mitologia, storia e futuro della più controversa risorsa del mondo*, Feltrinelli.

Mitchell, John V., Morita, Koji, Selley, Norman and Stern, Jonathan P. (2001) The new economy of oil: impacts on business, geopolitics and society, Royal Institute of international affairs.

Noreng, Oystein (2006) *Crude Power: Politics and the Oil Market*, I.B. Tauris Publishers.

OECD environmental outlook to 2030 (2008) OECD.

OECD Factbook 2009: Economic, Environmental and Social Statistics (2009) OECD.

Oil market report, IEA, edizioni 2008 e 2009.

OPEC Bulletin, OPEC, varie edizioni 2008 e 2009.

Simone, Piero De (2009) Il mercato dei carburanti: evoluzione normativa e prospettive, Conferenza Unione Petrolifera.

Speight, J.G. (1999) *The Chemistry and Technology of Petroleum*, Marcel Dekker.

Statistiche economiche energetiche e petrolifere (2008) Unione Petrolifera.

Van Der Linde, Coby (2000) *The State and the International Oil Market: Competition and the Changing Ownership of Crude Oil Assets*, Springer.

World Oil and Gas Review 2008, Eni, 2008.

Yergin, Daniel (1991) *The Prize: The Epic Quest for Oil, Money, & Power*, Simon & Schuster.

Index

Note: Page references in *italics* refer to Figures; those in **bold** refer to Tables.